CREATING ENGAGING DISCUSSIONS

CREATING ENGAGING DISCUSSIONS

Strategies for "Avoiding Crickets" in Any Size Classroom and Online

Jennifer H. Herman and Linda B. Nilson

Foreword by Stephen D. Brookfield

STERLING, VIRGINIA

Published by Stylus Publishing, LLC.
22883 Quicksilver Drive
Sterling, Virginia 20166-2102

Library of Congress Cataloging-in-Publication Data
Names: Herman, Jennifer H., 1979- editor. |
Nilson, Linda Burzotta, editor.
Title: Creating engaging discussions strategies for "avoiding crickets"
in any size classroom and online / edited by Jennifer H. Herman and
Linda B. Nilson; foreword by Stephen D. Brookfield.
Description: Sterling, Virginia : Stylus Publishing, LLC, [2018] |
Includes bibliographical references and index.
Identifiers: LCCN 2017039900 (print) |
LCCN 2017060672 (ebook) |
ISBN 9781620365618 (Library networkable e-edition) |
ISBN 9781620365625 (Consumer e-edition) |
ISBN 9781620365601 (pbk. : alk. paper) |
ISBN 9781620365595 (cloth : alk. paper)
Subjects: LCSH: Group work in education. | Discussion--Study and
teaching. | Inquiry-based learning. | Forums (Discussion and debate) |
Classroom management.
Classification: LCC LB1032 (ebook) |
LCC LB1032 .C69 2018 (print) |
DDC 371.39/5--dc23
LC record available at https://lccn.loc.gov/2017039900

13-digit ISBN: 978-1-62036-559-5 (cloth)
13-digit ISBN: 978-1-62036-560-1 (paperback)
13-digit ISBN: 978-1-62036-561-8 (library networkable e-edition)
13-digit ISBN: 978-1-62036-562-5 (consumer e-edition)

Printed in the United States of America

All first editions printed on acid-free paper
that meets the American National Standards Institute
Z39-48 Standard.

Bulk Purchases
Quantity discounts are available for use in workshops and for
staff development.
Call 1-800-232-0223

First Edition, 2018

To my father, my grandmother, and my teachers, for instilling in me a love of writing

To Greg, for his support over so many years

CONTENTS

QUICK REFERENCE TO DISCUSSION ACTIVITIES DESCRIBED IN THIS BOOK

Because this book contains so many discussion activities, we have organized them by purpose in the tables that follow to help readers. The first table lists and describes the activities that serve the purpose of motivating students to prepare for discussion; the second table, those that encourage students to listen actively; the third, those that increase or broaden student participation; and so on. We list the various purposes here. Many activities serve multiple purposes.

- To motivate preparation
- To encourage active listening
- To increase or broaden participation
- To improve the quality of contributions
- To assess participation
- To assess learning

To Motivate Preparation

Discussion Activity	Description	Book Page(s)
Written homework on assigned reading (or video, podcast)	Students bring in a summary of key points; questions; answers to study or reflective questions; quotations; an outline; a double journal of public and private reactions; or passages they see as central, puzzling, novel, interesting, or provocative. Usually worth credit but not graded.	12, 15
Discussion on discussion	Students discuss the elements of a good discussion and the qualities of a good discussion participant.	13–14
Change-your-mind debate	Students prepare and deliver a compelling, evidence-based argument for either the side they select or the opposing side to sway a "neutral" group, which is charged with asking each side challenging questions.	18
Simulation debate	Students role-play different positions with varying points of view or interests.	19
Prepared answers to discussion questions	You provide discussion questions before class and ask students to prepare answers as homework. For small-group work, members select the best answers as a group.	15
Deliberative dialogue	Students write analyses and appraisals of the positions in the readings. In class, they systematically share and listen to different ideas and points of view and then consider and evaluate the various sides.	36, 71–80

To Encourage Active Listening

Discussion Activity	Description	Book Page(s)
Note-taking on discussion	Students take notes on discussion, which works best if you scaffold by pointing out important milestones and integrating discussion material into quizzes, exams, and assignments.	17
Reporting out	One small-group member gives an oral summary of the group discussion (progress, conclusions, or answers), which works best if you randomly call on a few groups and randomly select the spokesperson within each group.	17
One-minute paper	Students write responses to one or more reflective prompts, such as (a) the most important, valuable, or useful thing(s) they learned during the discussion; (b) the most unexpected or surprising thing(s) they learned; or (c) the material they found most confusing.	17, 112
Fishbowl	A smaller group of students discusses a topic while a larger group quietly listens for understanding and may take notes. The larger group summarizes the smaller group's ideas and builds on them when the groups switch roles.	19
Comment summarizing	You ask a student to summarize and build on another student's contribution.	17, 20
Deliberative dialogue	See "To Motivate Preparation."	36, 71–80

To Increase or Broaden Participation

Discussion Activity	Description	Book Page(s)
Reporting out	See "To Encourage Active Listening."	17
One-minute paper	See "To Encourage Active Listening."	17, 112
Discussion on discussion	See "To Motivate Preparation."	13–14
Gallery walk (rotating stations)	You place sheets of paper around the room, each with a different prompt (e.g., question, problem, brainstorming task, graphic to draw) and assign four to five students to each sheet of paper. You give the groups three to five minutes to respond to the prompt individually or as a group. Then the groups rotate to a new sheet/prompt and repeat the process, generating new responses. After all groups visit each sheet, they walk around the "gallery" to read and comment on all the responses.	18–20
Change-your-mind debate	See "To Motivate Preparation."	18–20
Simulation debate	See "To Motivate Preparation."	19–20
Fishbowl	See "To Encourage Active Listening."	19–20
Focused listing	Students brainstorm a list of ideas, solutions, examples, and so on.	19
Thinking time	Students write down their ideas or reflect for 10 to 15 seconds before responding to a prompt.	20
Group summarizer	Assign an active listener in each small group to summarize others' ideas back to the group.	20
Comment summarizing	See "To Encourage Active Listening."	17, 20
Prepared answers to discussion questions	See "To Motivate Preparation."	15, 20
Concrete deliverables	Students formulate a specific number of concrete deliverables (e.g., three examples) in one to three minutes. In small groups, they then discuss and select three examples to report to the class. This works well in large-class polls.	20

Discussion Activity	Description	Book Page(s)
Snowball (with brainstorming)	You and your students toss a crumpled piece of paper around the room. The student who catches it or is closest to where it falls must respond to the brainstorming prompt.	32
Round-robin (with brainstorming)	You go around the room from student to student or group to group to solicit one new response to a brainstorming prompt. You should record each response where the whole class can see it.	21
Rotating facilitator	Near the end of the discussion, you ask a student to lead a discussion of "What haven't we said yet?"	21
Chalk talks	Students brainstorm in groups at the whiteboard.	25
Stand where you stand	Students stand in a corner of the room that represents their position on an issue. If each corner represents a different theoretical or analytical lens, students discuss an idea through the lens to which they are physically closest.	25
Folding line	Students arrange themselves along a line symbolizing a continuum of positions on a question or controversy. When the line "folds," those on one extreme make up a group with those on the other extreme, and they discuss or debate the issue. Or students can argue the other side's perspective and/or the extreme groups can try to persuade the "middle" group.	25
Role-play or simulation with debriefing	Some or all students participate in a role-play or simulation (the rest observe) and discuss their answers to debriefing questions.	25
Jigsaw	Students discuss a specialized topic in small groups of budding "experts" and then move into new groups, each with one representative of each of the expert groups, to teach their specialty.	25–26
Graphics	Students draw graphics (e.g., concept map, flowchart, matrix, concept circle diagram) to explain and discuss their organization of a body of knowledge.	26–28
Novel or outside-of-class stimuli	Students search for outside information or write about a personal experience related to the course material. They share and discuss their information or reflections in class.	28–30
Pinch points	In pairs or small groups, students discuss especially challenging new concepts (pinch points) during lecture breaks, particularly their understanding of the concepts and the place of these concepts in the lecture organization.	29

Discussion Activity	Description	Book Page(s)
Students' reactions to others' contributions	Students give their reactions, appraisals, extensions, qualifications, paraphrases, and the like to other students' contribution while you, as discussion moderator/facilitator, resist commenting.	30
Anonymous contributions	Students anonymously register or post their responses to private, sensitive, or controversial questions using sticky notes, anonymously submitted written answers, Web- or app-based polling tools, anonymous discussion boards, or chat rooms. Anonymity encourages honesty and reduces anxiety.	32
Card swapping, snowball tossing	Students anonymously write a question or response on a 3-inch-by-5-inch card and continuously swap cards for about 30 seconds to ensure that no one knows the origin of a given card. Alternatively, students use a piece of paper, crumple it up, toss it across the room, and retrieve someone else's crumpled paper. Students then share the question or comment on their new card or "snowball" in the discussion.	32
Three-penny rule	Give talkative students three pennies. They have to turn in a penny for each comment they make and can no longer comment when out of pennies.	20, 35
Three-student rule	A student who contributes cannot speak again until at least three other students have contributed.	35
Opening activities	• Students summarize the last class. • Students explain the purpose of an event that happened during the last class, such as a demonstration, role-play, video, or debate. • Students answer easy recall questions on the assigned readings or other homework. • Students describe how they reacted emotionally to the assigned readings or other homework. • Students write a response to a substantive or reflective question on the assigned readings or other homework. • Students brainstorm what they already know about a topic or what outcomes they expect of an experiment or a situation.	36

Discussion Activity	Description	Book Page(s)
Stimulation activities	• One or more students read key text passages aloud and explain why these passages are important. • Students argue against a controversial question or position that you state. • Students reflect on and write their reaction to a provocative statement. • Students form small groups to answer questions. • Students engage in conversation before responding.	36
Participation money	You judge the value of a given comment and explain why you gave it the value you did, teaching students what constitutes high- and low-quality contributions.	38
Real participation money	You start the course by paying students a quarter for every good-faith contribution. After a few classes, you reward only the first contribution of the day, then only the higher quality comments. Finally, you eliminate the quarters and reserve a $10 bill for an outstanding contribution.	38
Directing questions	Direct some questions to individual students or sectors of the room that have been quiet.	40
Private encouragement and rehearsal	Invite quiet students into your office hours and encourage them to participate. Give them a discussion prompt you'd like them to respond to during the next class and have them rehearse their answer with you.	40
Online extension	Extend classroom discussion to an online forum.	40
Discussion of ground rules	You and/or your students set expectations for interactions early in the course, especially for discussing sensitive subjects that may arise. You may do this verbally or in your syllabus or written grading criteria, or you may prefer to involve students in collaboratively developing ground rules or a course contract.	44–45
Explicit instructions for asynchronous online discussion	You choose topics or questions that closely connect with learning objectives, give clear directions for posts (e.g., integrate with the readings), assess contributions against well-defined criteria, and set ground rules for interaction. You can also assign rotating "starter" and "wrapper" roles, ask students to generate prompts or test questions, and gently keep the discussion on track.	49

Discussion Activity	Description	Book Page(s)
Participation log	At the beginning of the course, inform your students that they will be recording and evaluating their contributions. On a form you distribute, students report specifically what and when they contributed to class and how their contribution advanced learning. Request two self-assessments during the course in which students identify their strengths and ways to improve both the quantity and quality of their participation.	67–68
Participation portfolio	At the beginning of the course, inform your students that they will be recording and evaluating their contributions using a participation rubric you have developed or adopted. Every two to four weeks, students submit in writing a number of examples—two, three, or four, your choice—of their best contributions or replies and give them a collective grade, which you can then accept, raise, or lower.	67–68
Deliberative dialogue	See "To Motivate Preparation."	36, 71–80
Synchronous discussions via chat and webcam	Students honor a participation grading rubric, which you use to provide abundant feedback and encouragement. They also identify key takeaways in a class poll.	83–84
Collaborative autoethnography	Students follow a six-stage process focused around their own reflective prompts, acting as researchers using their personal stories as data to analyze in a broader social and relational context.	93
Mindful and contemplative informal writing	Students write a response to a complex prompt during the first 7 to 10 minutes of every class.	103
Chat and write	Students chat with others and write their responses before contributing publicly.	111
Research-centered labs	Students use lab sessions to conduct and discuss their authentic research.	115–116
Project-centered online discussions	Students use the online discussion forum to discuss their own field or research projects.	124–126

To Improve the Quality of Contributions

Discussion Activity	Description	Book Page(s)
Discussion on discussion	See "To Motivate Preparation."	13–14
Gallery walk (rotating stations)	See "To Increase or Broaden Participation."	18–20
Thinking time	See "To Increase or Broaden Participation."	20
Prepared answers to discussion questions	See "To Motivate Preparation."	15
Concrete deliverables	See "To Increase or Broaden Participation."	20
Jigsaw	See "To Increase or Broaden Participation."	25–26
Graphics	See "To Increase or Broaden Participation."	26–28
Participation money	See "To Increase or Broaden Participation."	38
Real participation money	See "To Increase or Broaden Participation."	38
Explicit instructions for asynchronous online discussion	See "To Increase or Broaden Participation."	49
Participation log	See "To Increase or Broaden Participation."	67–68
Participation portfolio	See "To Increase or Broaden Participation."	67–68
Deliberative dialogue	See "To Motivate Preparation."	36, 71–80
Synchronous discussions via chat and webcam	See "To Increase or Broaden Participation."	83–84
Collaborative autoethnography	See "To Increase or Broaden Participation."	92
Mindful and contemplative informal writing	See "To Increase or Broaden Participation."	101
Chat and write	See "To Increase or Broaden Participation."	107
Research-centered labs	See "To Increase or Broaden Participation."	114
Project-centered online discussions	See "To Increase or Broaden Participation."	121

To Assess Participation

Discussion Activity	Description	Book Page(s)
Students' written evaluations	Students write evaluations of (a) the degree of community in the class, (b) the overall class participation (look for the collective class opinion), or (c) their own discussion contributions (provide criteria), plus improvement strategies.	64
Participation log	See "To Increase or Broaden Participation."	67–68
Participation portfolio	See "To Increase or Broaden Participation."	67–68

To Assess Learning

Discussion Activity	Description	Book Page(s)
Pretest/posttest knowledge or confidence	Students write answers to a question about their level of knowledge or confidence on the day's topic at the beginning and end of class.	65
Written response	Students write or post online their answer to an important question related to the discussion at the end of the session.	65
Written evaluations	Students evaluate the quality of the discussion in terms of how it solved a problem, handled a conflict, reached a goal, or changed their understanding or thinking. They may need a rubric from you.	65
Reflection on change	Students informally write responses to prompts asking how their thinking or understanding changed or deepened due to the discussion.	65
Takeaways	Students write or post their list of takeaways from the discussion.	65
Papers	Students write papers drawing on their pre- or postdiscussion learning journal.	65

Discussion Activity	Description	Book Page(s)
Classroom assessment technique (CAT)	Students complete a CAT appropriate to the discussion topic, such as a one-minute paper, four-square, focused listing, application cards, or muddiest point.	66
Reflection on benefits from assignment	Students write reflections on how they benefited from the major assignment on which discussions focused.	66
Reflection on gains from discussions	Students write reflections on what they gained from face-to-face and online discussions with an emphasis on their sense of class community, their ability to integrate the discussions across platforms, and their perceived depth of understanding of course concepts.	66
Short-essay quiz	After a discussion, students take a short-essay quiz that assesses how well they achieved your ultimate objective(s). Inform them about the objective(s) and quiz in advance.	66

FOREWORD

If you're reading this book, you probably regard a good discussion as the crown jewel of your pedagogy. However, to mix metaphors appallingly, it is often a unicorn, a creature only of mythology or alternate universes. I ran my first college discussion in 1970, and five decades later I'm still struggling to glimpse that unicorn. Occasionally I see the horn peeping around my classroom door, but I know this creature of the forest is easily startled. A wrongly worded question or a bungled attempt to call on a student, and it's vanished deep into the undergrowth.

Of course, that's not to say I don't have a lot of classroom discussions in which people talk a lot; I do. The room is often full of sound, and sometimes fury, particularly when I hold discussions around contentious topics. But verbal speech alone does not good discussion make. Indeed, I'd go so far as to say that my best discussions usually have long periods of silence. For me a lot of silence is one of the chief indicators that learning is happening in a discussion. As a student I hated being coerced into speech in a discussion, and the desire to avoid students feeling as though they are being surveilled for the number of words they put into the air has been an important element in how I've constructed my own practice of discussion. I don't want learning to be sabotaged by the performance anxiety of students wondering, "Do I sound smart enough? Have I spoken the requisite number of times?"

Despite my personal experiences as a student, when I'm a teacher and the air is full of uninterrupted talk, it's easy for me to feel triumphant. I can say to myself, "Wow, these students are *so* interested in the topic, they can't wait to get a word in. What a fantastically engaged classroom I've created!" But then I stop and think about the discussions that I've learned the most from, and it's clear that they involved a lot of careful listening. For example, any discussion in which people are articulating viewpoints that challenge my previous understanding requires me to understand complex points and open myself up to hearing unfamiliar perspectives. As an elderly White man who has been in and facilitated many discussions about racism and White supremacy, I know that I spend a lot of time thinking and processing. I'm often receiving information that explodes my White assumptions about how the world operates and presents me with a starkly different, brutal reality. In discussions like these, I'm mulling over new information, thinking through challenging comments, creating meaning from alternative ideas, dealing with my immediate emotional responses, and contextualizing abstract theory by making links to my own experiences.

So silence is not the enemy of discussion. In fact, it's a crucial conversational dynamic that allows people to do the kinds of things I outlined previously. Sometimes crickets chirping is the necessary and inevitable soundtrack to deep learning. But then there are the crickets whose sound dominates the room for all the wrong reasons. Here the deafening sound of chirping signifies only the presence of confusion or apathy in participants and tells us that no real learning is happening. Jennifer Herman and Linda Nilson's terrific book is written for rooms infested with those kinds of crickets.

This book is split into two halves. In the first half, the coauthors guide us through some common concerns and projects of those who teach through discussion. They consider how to engage everyone, avoid common pitfalls, connect discussion to learning, and gauge the effectiveness of a particular discussion. These chapters are stuffed with techniques, suggestions, exercises, and activities that can be adapted to multiple settings. In the second half, we find eight case studies that illustrate approaches to holding good discussions across the disciplines. To concretize the application of discussion strategies in this way is enormously helpful.

I have often argued that teachers are good burglars. In my own case my practice has been built on theft. If I see someone doing something interesting I ask myself, "Can I copy that? What would the imitation look like in my own classroom?" When I read about a new teaching activity I wonder how I can steal it and reshape it for my own context. This is one reason why I put all of my own techniques, exercises, and activities up on my own home page and urge people to steal from it. If you have a mind, check it out at www.stephenbrookfield.com and steal what seems useful. In reality, it's not stealing because I give you my permission.

I've stolen a lot from this book. I regard myself as an avid collector of new pedagogic baubles and love it when I stumble across a new way to engage my students as I have done many times by reading Herman and Nilson's work. I have no doubt that as you read this book your own collection of discussion-based teaching strategies will be significantly enlarged. But don't keep them stored in a safe or vault—bring them into your class and use them!

Stephen D. Brookfield
University of St. Thomas,
Minneapolis-St. Paul, Minnesota

PREFACE

Whether face-to-face or online, perhaps nothing satisfies a faculty member like having led a productive discussion—one in which all students were engaged and their learning met all the hoped-for objectives. The instructor can leave the classroom or close the discussion board glowing with a sense of success.

How often does this happen, though? How often are even most of the students passionately involved? How often do well-considered learning objectives guide the discussion? For that matter, how does an instructor even know how much student engagement and learning has occurred?

For being such a mainstay teaching method, discussion has inspired surprisingly few resources to help faculty maximize its learning value, whether face-to-face or online. Recently, we've seen Brookfield and Preskill's (2016) *The Discussion Book: 50 Great Ways to Get People Talking*, following their 2005 book, *Discussion as a Way of Teaching: Tools and Techniques for Democratic Classrooms*, (2nd edition). The former briefly describes 50 techniques taken from their earlier books and workshop materials, and the latter blends a philosophy of discussion as a reflection of democracy with an assortment of ways to generate and moderate student participation. Brookfield and Preskill's discussion strategies tailor well in small, face-to-face classes, but not so much in large or online classes. Howard's (2015) *Discussion in the College Classroom* adopts a sociological point of view in synthesizing the research on classroom discussion and drawing out the implications for practice. To a modest degree, it addresses the online context. However, all of these books focus on only one facet of discussion, student participation, which does not guarantee student learning.

Other books that examine discussion do so only briefly within a wide range of other college teaching methods, and these similarly emphasize getting students to talk—for example, Barkley's *Student Engagement Techniques: A Handbook for College Faculty* (2015); Barkley, Major, and Cross's *Collaborative Learning Techniques: A Handbook for College Faculty* (2014); and Nilson's *Teaching at Its Best: A Research-Based Resource for College Instructors* (2016).

Indeed, as educational developers over many years, we have observed the faculty's struggle to design and facilitate classroom and online discussions that engage all learners; it is one of the most prevalent and consistent challenges instructors face. So many times, we have watched instructors pose a provocative, carefully constructed discussion question only to be met by silence. We imagined the sound of crickets echoing through the classroom as the instructor waited uncomfortably for a student to break the tension and finally respond. Unfortunately, just one session of crickets can infest the spirit of a class for an entire term.

But participation is not the only challenge: Talk alone is cheap. Just as important, how can you create a discussion that offers students a valuable learning experience, one that explores the content and facilitates learning in a deep, meaningful way? Plus, how do you know how effective the discussion has been? How can you assess it?

Creating Engaging Discussions: Strategies for "Avoiding Crickets" in Any Size Classroom and Online offers answers to these crucial questions. It is organized around identifying, analyzing, and solving common problems in both classroom and online discussions and in both small and large classes. In the first chapter, we use short cases to illustrate some of the most common challenges. Then, taking a direct, practice-oriented approach, we focus on ways to move beyond these challenges. We emphasize principles, design, techniques, and cases that demonstrate the day-to-day application of the principles. We apply familiar course design processes to construct effective discussion sessions.

We favor cases to elucidate many of our points. We feature eight short case studies in which faculty members from a wide range of disciplines present the strategies they have designed or adapted and implemented in their face-to-face, blended, or online courses at the undergraduate or graduate level. These instructors have successfully increased student engagement and learning using these strategies and have conducted assessments to prove it. The authors open their cases describing the original pedagogical challenge they faced and proceed to explain how they addressed it and assessed the results of their innovation. They also offer practical recommendations to readers who may want to try their strategies.

Selecting these 8 cases proved to be a difficult, hair-splitting process. We received almost 40 submissions from a call for proposals we issued on the discussion group of the Professional and Organizational Development (POD) Network in Higher Education and the electronic mailing list of the Educational Developers Caucus (EDC) of the Canada-based Society for Teaching and Learning in Higher Education (STLHE). We requested that POD and STLHE-EDC members share the call with their faculty. We also extended the call to instructors at our own institutions, Simmons College and Clemson University. Our criteria for selecting cases included the innovativeness of the discussion technique and the rigor of the assessment; we also aimed to represent a range of disciplines, course levels, and delivery platforms.

Obviously, our primary audience is faculty members who teach courses that use, or could use, discussion and seek to create both engaging and effective face-to-face and online exchanges. Our recommendations apply across disciplines and course levels, as well as to varied class sizes. We intend to fill the need for a resource that guides faculty of all ranks and institutional types in designing, facilitating, and assessing not only engaging but also learning-rich discussions.

We also speak to educational developers, who can use this resource in their programs and private consultations. At the graduate level, this book can serve as a text or workshop resource in college teaching courses and teaching assistant development programs. To facilitate group learning, the final chapter provides a set of resources and activities for faculty and graduate students who are reading the book as a group and educational developers who lead such groups. We include discussion questions on the case studies, writing prompts, and jigsaw formats—all designed to engage a reading group more fully with the material.

Jennifer H. Herman,
Boston, MA
September 2017

Linda B. Nilson,
Anderson, SC
September 2017

ACKNOWLEDGMENTS

John von Knorring, president of Stylus Publishing, is everything you want in a publisher: ready to offer wise counsel and creative ideas, but flexible; quick to respond to inquiries; thorough in his answers and advice; knowledgeable about the market; and always diplomatic in his critiques. Of course, without his approval, this book would not exist. So, we thank John for believing in our proposal and our ability to deliver on our promises.

We thank our contributors for all their hard work writing up their classroom and online experiences in leading discussions, from the letdowns to the successes. We keep too many of our teaching practices private and applaud our contributors for the courage they displayed in candidly sharing theirs:

- Mary Ann Drury, Columbia University
- Mary Jo Festle, Elon University
- Matthea Marquart, Columbia University
- Mary Shapiro, Simmons College
- Jennifer W. Shewmaker, Abilene Christian University
- Billy Strean, University of Alberta
- Heather Townsend, Community College of Rhode Island
- Janelle DeCarrico Voegele, Portland State University
- David M. Wilson, Parkland College

Jennifer H. Herman thought about the concept for this book for more than a year before moving forward, and she has her close friend Heather McEntarfer of SUNY Fredonia to thank for helping her think through the book's scope and focus. She also thanks Linda for being such a wise, candid, and reliable coauthor throughout this process—a delight to work with is an understatement; thank you for your willingness to partner on this project and for bringing your years of experience to this text. Thank you also to the participants at the 2016 POD conference roundtable discussion; several of the ideas shared at that session ended up being incorporated into this text. Thank you also to Jennifer's colleagues at Simmons for their support and feedback throughout the writing process, and to Steve, Jennifer's husband, for his patience, love, and for giving her uninterrupted quiet when she needed it.

Linda B. Nilson thanks Jennifer for asking her to coauthor this book. It was all Jennifer's brilliant vision from its very conception to the organization and chapter outlines to the idea of soliciting real cases and synthesizing our faculty development experience to develop illustrative ones. Linda jumped at the chance to work with someone as professional, creative, and just plain smart as Jennifer.

Thanks are also due the spring 2016 and spring 2017 writing groups for inspiring and encouraging Linda's progress on this book. She facilitated the former group for Clemson University faculty and graduate students, and English lecturer and poet Mike Pulley led the latter. She is gratified that her writing groups continue after her retirement from Clemson.

Having written several books on his "watch," Linda is running out of different ways to express her gratitude to her husband, Greg Bauernfeind. He consistently gives his wholehearted support to all her professional endeavors and tolerates her endless hours burrowed away in her office. And so she rightfully dedicates her work on the book to him.

I

THE STRENGTHS
AND CHALLENGES OF
DISCUSSION

Jennifer H. Herman and Linda B. Nilson

B efore we evaluate *discussion*, let's identify what it is. The following various definitions may come to mind:

- an exchange of different interpretations, explanations, approaches to a problem, or possible solutions, followed by an evaluation;
- a collective analysis of arguments or claims;
- the expression of varying opinions, positions, or perspectives, along with justifications; and
- a student-active, constructivist teaching method in which students construct new knowledge based on their experience and prior knowledge in the process of expressing their thoughts.

All of these are correct; each captures a different facet of the interaction. In fact, defining *discussion* is a good topic for discussion because the activity has multiple respectable viewpoints and invites their expression.

Recitation Versus Discussion

By contrast, *recitation* involves answering questions that call for restating knowledge, terms, or facts that learners should be able to remember from reading or hearing about them. Even an ardent constructivist would agree that some factual, conceptual, procedural, and metacognitive knowledge must become second nature to a learner, whether through memorization, experience, or repeated use. Although not as stimulating as a good discussion, recitation serves several important purposes:

- It provides students with retrieval practice of key material that they need to be able to recall.
- It gives them practice in speaking the language of the discipline (Leamnson, 1999).
- It gives them the opportunity to express knowledge in their own words and assess their understanding.
- It prepares them for discussion by ensuring they have the material they will need at their fingertips.

Recitation requires little more preparation than reviewing recent class sessions and assigned readings, videos, or podcasts and developing some straightforward questions about some key points. Because students should be ready to answer these questions, many instructors feel free to cold-call on individuals rather than choose from among raised hands. They might also "grade" responses acceptable/unacceptable and give a participation point for an acceptable answer. Although students may phrase their answers differently, recitation questions have only one correct response, unless that response has more than one part and you are willing to accept just one from each student. For instance, you might say, "The chapter gives three reasons for spikes in the suicide rate. What's one of them?"

Discussion presents more challenges. It is not a simple matter of asking a question and students answering it. If the answers aren't "in the book," then the questions aren't either. In fact, the most vapid discussions are unintended recitation sessions, which aren't discussions at all. Discussion questions have a number of different valid responses, and brainstorm questions may have many. In addition to some recall, they demand higher level thinking—cognitive operations like interpretation, induction, deduction, application, analysis, inference, generalization, fuzzy problem-solving, evaluation, conclusion drawing, or creativity. In other words, they go beyond the provided material, and you can't anticipate all the answers students may give.

Where might you find such questions? Although test banks and instructor guides may supply recitation questions, only rarely do these furnish good discussion questions. You're usually on your own to formulate them.

The sources of recitation questions (classes, readings, etc.) usually suggest a logical order for asking the questions: the order in which the material appears. So you normally pose questions on the first part of the class session, chapter, video, or podcast first, those on the second part next, and so on. But with discussion, you usually have, or *should* have, a destination in mind— that is, one or more ultimate questions that students couldn't answer at the beginning of the session but can by the end. Think of yourself as leading students on a cognitive trip that occasionally evokes emotions such as surprise, curiosity, excitement, empathy, and even discomfort and winds up in some mental place that students haven't been before.

As on any trip, things can go wrong during a discussion. The class can get lost, go off track, or wind up going nowhere. You may not have mapped out the trip adequately or defined a destination well enough. We illustrate the pitfalls in scenarios we have observed in actual classes. As the next section shows, naïvely disregarding these land mines leads to negative consequences for you, your students, and the success of your course.

So is it really worth the effort to plan out and be prepared to moderate a good discussion? Is the method worth the risks?

Why the Challenges Are Worth the Risk: The Strengths of Discussion

Discussion can pay off handsomely. It shines brightest when the learning objectives ascend to higher level thinking. Of course, this is assuming that the person leading and moderating the discussion—usually the instructor but can be a student—has planned and is managing it wisely. Under these favorable conditions, discussion fosters complex thought, questioning, communication, interest, and retention, enhancing skills such as the following (Bligh, 2000; Bonwell & Eison, 1991; Brookfield & Preskill, 2005; Dallimore, Hertenstein, & Platt, 2008, 2016; Delaney, 1991; Ewens, 2000; Forster, Hounsell, & Thompson, 1995; Gilmore & Schall, 1996; Howard, 2015; Kustra & Potter, 2008; Lakey, 2010; Lempert, Xavier, & DeSouza, 1995; McKeachie, 2002; B.D. Robinson & Schaible, 1993; Springer, Stanne, & Donovan, 1999):

- active listening;
- analysis and evaluation of arguments and positions;
- citizenship;
- clarification of the material;
- confirmation of one's understanding;
- critical examination of one's attitudes, beliefs, behaviors, and values;
- critical thinking;
- deep, conceptual understanding;
- engagement;
- exposure to new perspectives (e.g., those of diverse learners and introverts);

- integration of ideas;
- long-term retention of the subject matter;
- motivation to learn more about the subject matter;
- open-mindedness to new ideas and viewpoints;
- oral communication;
- problem-solving (related to cases, problematic situations, ethical dilemmas, unexpected results, and creative challenges as well as mathematical problems);
- retention of the material; and
- transfer of knowledge to new contexts.

Many of these learning benefits have an affective component. Citizenship, for example, carries a sense of duty to and participation in one's community and society. This sense of duty in turn presumes values such as loyalty, optimism, affinity, and humanity. Motivation to learn more implies emotions such as curiosity, appreciation, enjoyment, and desire. Open-mindedness and self-examination thrive together and can involve surprise and discomfort in the face of new ideas, especially when they challenge a learner's current way of thinking and acting. Discussion also requires interacting with others, and each individual probably arouses positive, negative, or mixed feelings.

Whatever they may be, emotions bring additional neurotransmitters into the learning process, augmenting the likelihood and ease of storage and retrieval of the cognitive material (Leamnson, 1999, 2000). In general, neurotransmitters are biochemicals that travel across a synapse to bind to receptor cells on the postsynaptic membrane, ultimately changing the electric state of the cells by inhibiting or exciting them (Lahey & Rosen, 2014). Dopamine, for example, comes into play when the learning is enjoyable, exciting, or fun, and it acts as a brain auto-save feature. Serotonin is produced by friendships, which discussion and group work can foster. Norepinephrine (or noradrenaline) is stimulated by competitive games and simulations (Georgic, 2015), which may serve as topics for debriefing discussions.

We cannot emphasize enough that the learning benefits of discussion accrue only when instructors know how to plan and lead one effectively. Research warns us that although active learning enhances student performance (Freeman et al., 2014) it does so only when an instructor implements it following the best practices laid out in the literature (Andrews, Leonard, Colgrove, & Kalinowski, 2011). Otherwise, a method like discussion can fail, as the next section shows.

The Typical Pitfalls and Risks of Discussion

The following cases illustrate some of the ways that discussions can go awry.

Case 1: Evolutionary Biology

It's the first day of class of her new course, and Professor Hu has just finished reviewing her policies and expectations of her students. She has set high standards because almost all of her students are biology majors. She is eager to get into the subject matter.

"You've all completed at least one biology course, and some of you have taken several. So you should know the answer to this first question. What is science?"

She scans her class of 35 and sees 70 eyes looking down at their desks. "Come on, folks, you're planning on becoming biologists or medical professionals. What is science?" She hopes she doesn't sound too impatient.

At least 10 seconds of crickets.

"Okay, what do scientists do in the lab?"

After several seconds, one student answers in a barely audible voice. "Run experiments."

"Yes, that's one thing they do. What else?" Not wanting to lose any more precious class time, she counts to five and says, "They make observations. They analyze materials. In biology, these materials are usually organic, perhaps part of an animal or plant from the field. So why is evolutionary biology considered to be a science?"

Another student seems a bit agitated and speaks up. "I took botany and zoology, and I see why they're sciences. But I don't think evolution is because it's just a theory, and you can't run experiments to prove it."

Professor Hu jumps in to defend her field. "Evolution is overwhelmingly supported by scientific evidence. Biologists have found ancient fossils of animals related to today's species. They've found similar DNA structures across similar species. They've observed adaptive genetic changes in species like fruit flies that reproduce rapidly."

Another student cuts her off. "Yeah, well, I'm not a fruit fly."

Yet another student chimes in, "I don't believe in evolution."

And another, "I took this course to bear witness to my faith against evolution. Intelligent design makes a lot more sense."

"But where's the scientific evidence for intelligent design?" Professor Hu responds.

The class goes quiet again, until a student in the back row says in an accusatory tone, "You didn't warn us that we'd have to give up our religion to pass this course. You were supposed to give us a trigger warning."

Case 2: Contemporary American Politics

Professor Reter is feeling optimistic as the students in his Contemporary American Politics course arrange their desks into circles with six students each. He had asked them to bring in an example of an editorial or website that demonstrates reporting bias against one of the presidential candidates. His hope is that they can develop a deeper understanding of how choices around the selection and presentation of evidence can sway public opinion.

"Once you're in your groups," he says, "please introduce yourselves. Because we have such a large class, you might not all know each other. When you are ready to start, please take turns sharing your articles. Explain how you know that the article is biased. What information in the article might be missing or misleading? Finally, what impact would this bias have on the reader's perception of the candidate? Please pick a person who will record and report out your group's main discussion points to the class. You have 20 minutes."

Immediately, conversation begins around the room, and Professor Reter is pleased that the discussion is off to a great start. As he moves from group to group listening in, though, he notices that nearly every student has brought in an article that is critical of the leading Democratic candidate, and much of the conversation is focused on refuting the authors' attacks on the candidate or complaining about the election in general, rather than looking for bias in the use of evidence in the articles. Professor Reter breaks into the conversation of several groups to help guide them back in the right direction, but it seems as though they are easily getting off track. He also notices several students talking at length about a specific Republican family member or acquaintance of theirs who would be easily swayed by the misinformation, rather than talking about a reader more generally. During the report-out session, the comments are brief because many of the groups forgot to record their ideas.

Concerned about how the discussion went, Professor Reter passes out index cards and asks each student to write down an example of bias that he or she uncovered in group discussion, an example of the impact on the reader's perception, and the student's thoughts on how the discussion went overall. He asks them to please not include their names and to drop them on the front table before leaving class.

To his dismay, the cards reveal that the students described the discussion as a "Republican-bashing session," a "waste of time," and "very uncomfortable." Some of the cards reveal an understanding of bias and its impact on perception, but most of the students seem to have missed the point of the discussion.

Case 3: Sociology Course on Collective Behavior

It's the middle of the class period, and Professor Ronkowski decides to begin a discussion on disaster behavior. It's an especially interesting topic, he reasons, because most of the findings run counter to the myths that the media have popularized about widespread looting, emotional breakdowns, and dog-eat-dog behavior.

He poses a question to his students, most of them sociology majors: "Why do you think the therapeutic community springs up in the immediate aftermath of a natural disaster?" During his several seconds of wait time, four hands go up, then five. Good sign, he thinks, and he starts to call on students by name.

> Tiffany: Perhaps it's a social survival reaction. People can't survive without other people, so they help each other.
>
> Josh: Yes, but people can't survive if too many other people survive because there aren't many resources.

Professor Ronkowski seizes on these conflicting remarks to lead into another question: "So how can you resolve the survival reaction with the resource shortage?"

> Julie: My uncle was in the Oklahoma City tornado, and he said the power went out and he couldn't get gas for four days. Then everyone had to wait in long lines and were really pissed off.
>
> Mark: My mom was living in New Orleans when Katrina hit, and there wasn't any ice available and her family's food spoiled. She said it was awful.
>
> Keisha: A friend of mine was in the flood in West Virginia. They lost power and Wi-Fi, and she was completely cut off from all her friends.

It seems that all the students have a personal story to share about someone they know living through a disaster. Then the discussion veers off onto the topic of being away from their cell phones and feeling isolated. The students are riveted, and some quiet ones are sharing, too, so Professor Ronkowski lets the exchange go on until the end of class. He's happy about the level of participation but disappointed that the discussion mostly reinforced disaster myths and wandered so far afield from his original question. He wonders what his students got out of the class.

Case 4: Special Topics Course on Utopian Literature

"Why do you think Candide argues for 'cultivating our garden' at the end of the novel? Has he become completely disillusioned with Pangloss's optimism? Or is he saying that it is possible to construct a type of Utopia, rather than assuming that one already exists?"

Professor Dowen asks the questions enthusiastically, then pauses, counting to 10 in her head to give her students time to answer. The 15 students in her special topics seminar Utopian Literature are sitting with their desks in a circle. This course is an elective for English majors, but most of the students in the course are not majors and are taking the course because it fulfills one of their general education distribution requirements. Professor Dowen is frustrated by how many of the students seemed disengaged from the first day of class and wonders whether the three majors in the class are just as frustrated by how few of their classmates seem to have actually read the novel.

Looking around the circle, Professor Dowen notices that most of the students are avoiding eye contact—either flipping through their rented copies of *Candide* or "taking notes." The atmosphere in the room grows increasingly awkward as the seconds of silence tick away. Janie and Michelle, two of the English majors in the course, are glancing around the circle, looking to see whether anyone else might speak up before they jump in as usual.

Finally, Janie says, "I think he's just completely disillusioned. He's suffered so much; he's just trying to survive as best as he can with the people most important to him."

Michelle nods. "Yes, I agree with Janie. He's just matured and is wiser after everything that he's been through, and he knows that it's better to build something than just expect everything to turn out okay." Janie just nods in agreement. A few more seconds tick by, but no one else speaks up.

Inside, Professor Dowen frowns. Not only is the conversation at a standstill again, but Michelle just contradicted Janie while stating that she agreed with her, and no one seemed to pick up on that.

"So what do the rest of you think?" she asks, looking around at the rest of the class. "Has Candide completely given up hope for a perfect life by the end, or does he think that he can build it for himself?"

She counts to 20, and there are some shrugs and murmurs of "given up." She asks, "Why do you think so?"

Janie says, "Well, like Michelle said—all of the horrible things he's been through," and the class nods in agreement, and there is silence again. Not sure how she can guide the students deeper, Professor Dowen moves on to her next prepared question.

The Impact on Students

When discussion fails, as it does in these scenarios, students lose more than a learning experience. They lose faith in the method itself. They come to see it as a bull session, a boring waste of time, an inefficient and ineffective way to learn, an activity not worth the effort to participate in. They may even find that it impedes their learning by adding confusion, especially when it results in no clear conclusions. Besides, why should they care about each other's perspectives and viewpoints when they are waiting to hear the authoritative (*your*) word? They believe, often correctly, that this is what they will be tested on, not the uninformed, impulsive opinions of their peers. On a more personal level, students who are quiet, introverted, dissenting, or unfamiliar with college classroom norms and expectations may feel marginalized, resentful, or drowned out by the small minority who jump to respond. They cannot and do not care to compete for the floor, so they tune out or get angry. They become part of the "silent majority" and are more than willing to relinquish their responsibility for the success of a discussion to a vocal few students. Sociologists call this normative pattern of classroom behavior the "consolidation of responsibility" (Howard, 2015, p. 12; Karp & Yoels, 1976, p. 430).

These bad perceptions and experiences make it less likely that students will bother to pay attention and contribute to the next discussion session in any course. They will adopt the norm of "civil attention," which means looking like they're paying attention when they're not (Howard, 2015, p. 11; Karp & Yoels, 1976, p. 438).

The Impact on Faculty

As illustrated in the stories presented previously, instructors who walk out of a failed discussion feel responsible, discouraged, and discredited. Their self-confidence sags. They may wonder what kind of imposter they are if they can't even lead a fruitful discussion, asking themselves what it takes to get their students talking, and why they don't know how to do it. If students do talk, they often want to shift the discussion to another topic. Instructors wonder what they are doing wrong and what their students must think of them, perhaps assuming maybe they are just not very good in the classroom or just don't have the charisma that discussion requires of an instructor. They may also worry about the effects of the bad experience on their students, especially the class dynamics and culture. Students won't want to get involved in a discussion again. They may not choose to participate in any class activities, whether a simulation, game, debate, or something else. As they withdraw and become passive, their learning is bound to suffer. So a concerned instructor may just reason, "Why try and fail again?"

Instructors may also wonder what their students actually gain from a discussion. Students want closure. They want to know what the right answers to the questions are and what will be on the next exam. Besides, how is an instructor supposed to find out what her students learned?

Few faculty members learn how to lead a discussion. They don't know how to stimulate broad and meaningful participation, how to keep a discussion open to student direction but on track, or how to assess a discussion.

They may not even understand that discussion is a technique with best practices that anyone can follow.

How This Book Catalogs and Remedies the Challenges of Discussion

If we examine the cases of failed discussions, they seem to delineate three areas of concern in both classroom and online discussions: (a) problematic student engagement, whether inappropriate, inconsistent, uneven, or lacking; (b) disconnect from the course content or advancing it; and (c) a lack of assessment. The first area presents social challenges because, as the instructor, you have to institute and enforce new norms and standards for active student attention and participation to replace the preexisting ones of civil attention and consolidation of responsibility (Howard, 2015; Karp & Yoels, 1976). The second area belies inadequate planning and control of the discussion. Although many faculty may not immediately see a need to address the third area, how else can instructors tell if a discussion served its purpose and whether they accomplished their objectives?

Each of these areas receives a chapter of its own in this book: In chapter 2, we present 12 principles of student behavior in discussion, each of which suggests strategies for creating engaging discussions with broad participation. In chapter 3, we recommend solutions to a host of common problems that can arise, from personal attacks to narcissistic comments to the deafening quiet of crickets. Chapter 4 lays out ways to ensure that discussions lead to worthwhile learning, specifically by integrating them into the course design and structuring them to help students achieve predetermined objectives. Chapter 5 focuses on how to assess the two facets of a discussion just addressed: (a) how well it engages students and stimulates their participation, and (b) how well it advances the course content. Such assessment need not involve grading.

Chapters 6 through 13 present actual case studies of successful classroom and online discussions across the disciplines at both the graduate and undergraduate levels. These were written by real instructors in response to a call we put out on electronic mailing lists of educational and faculty developers to distribute to their faculty. We received an overwhelming response to our call, making it very difficult to select just a few cases for this book. Rest assured that you will be reading the best of the best examples of participatory, productive, and effectively assessed discussions.

We expect that at least several faculty discussion groups will form around this book and several college teaching graduate courses will adopt it. Chapter 14 provides resources for such groups and courses in the form of questions and topics for exchange. No doubt graduate teaching assistants entrusted with laboratories, discussion sections, and their own courses will also find valuable advice in this book.

GETTING ALL
STUDENTS ENGAGED

Jennifer H. Herman and Linda B. Nilson

L et's consider the first reason that discussion can fail—problematic student engagement. Drawing on the teaching and learning literature, we propose 12 principles to guide class discussion. These principles incorporate the ways that student behavior typically impacts discussion, specifically the appropriateness, consistency, breadth, or frequency of student participation, whether in a classroom or online. We describe each of these principles as well as several potential strategies for improving student engagement. Of course, problems always crop up along the way when designing and facilitating successful discussions, and we suggest solutions to several common challenges in chapter 3.

12 Principles to Guide Class Discussion

Following are 12 principles to guide class discussion.

1. Students must be prepared for discussion.
2. Students must feel safe to express themselves.
3. Students need good reasons to listen actively.
4. Students respond well to a variety of structured discussion formats.
5. Students contribute as equally as the discussion structure requires.
6. Students respond well to questions with multiple good answers.
7. Students benefit from having time to think before contributing.
8. Students can benefit from expressing themselves in motion and space.
9. Students can benefit from expressing themselves graphically.
10. Students respond well to novel stimuli, such as outside ideas or research.

11. Students participate according to how effectively a discussion is moderated.
12. Students must see their personal value as separate from the value of their contributions.

We address each principle in turn, considering its importance to student engagement and the strategies it suggests for ensuring broad and fruitful student participation in discussion.

Principle 1: Students Must Be Prepared for Discussion

At the beginning of chapter 1, we listed some definitions of *discussion*. They all tied the activity to some form of debatable or uncertain knowledge, presumably in a discipline: interpretations, explanations, approaches or possible solutions to a problem, evaluations, arguments, claims, opinions, positions, or perspectives, along with justifications. In other words, discussion involves higher level thinking about some content. Students can't participate, let alone advance their learning, if they come into the classroom or forum knowing little or nothing about the discussion topic. They *have to* prepare for the occasion. If they have little or nothing to contribute, their self-confidence suffers and their fear of peer disapproval rises, which in turn reduces their self-reported participation (Roehling, Vander Kooi, Dykema, Quisenberry, & Vandlen, 2011; Weaver & Qi, 2005).

Research tells us that relatively few students do the assigned reading, which is the most common form of preparation, unless faculty hold them accountable with some form of reward or sanction, such as required homework, a quiz, recitation, or other class activity that figures at least modestly into their course grade (Burchfield & Sappington, 2000; Hoeft, 2012; Huang, Blacklock, & Capps, 2013; Nathan, 2005; Nilson, 2016). Therefore, first, institute some kind of compliance measure to induce student preparation for discussion. Although students may find podcasts and videos less odious than readings, you still have to hold students accountable for carefully processing them. Accountability strategies to ensure that students prepare also can include nongraded activities that might figure into a broader participation grade—for instance, bringing to class a written summary of key points, an outline, or questions from an assigned reading.

Second, students are more likely to complete preparatory assignments when they understand their purpose and their importance within the course (Talbert, 2017). Therefore, consider telling students how each reading, video, problem set, or other assignment will help them achieve one or more course outcomes or perform well on another assignment or upcoming exam.

Students can't figure this out on their own because they are unfamiliar with course design, pedagogy, and the broad overview of your course.

Similarly, students rarely understand the value of discussion and the importance of their participation, especially given that they are used to playing a passive role (Howard, 2015; Karp & Yoels, 1976). But a solid explanation from you should convince them that it's worth their while to prepare. On the first day of class, you might describe the purpose of discussion as the sharing and assessment of varied, defensible perspectives, along with the evidence behind them. Then connect this purpose to the workplace realities they are facing, as Talbert (2017) recommends for preparing students for flipped learning. In the workplace, students will have to discuss and debate conflicting interpretations of situations in a civil manner. They will confront unknowns, uncertainties, and competing approaches to complex problems without clear strategies for solving them. Textbook facts won't carry the day for them; practice and comfort in participating actively in engaging discussions will.

Of course, the topics for classroom discussion must allow for legitimate discrepancies in perspective; they must contain elements of uncertainty or controversy. Agreement may feel good, but learning takes place around the *differences* in approaches and positions, the *dis*agreements and the dissimilar directions that minds can take. Even discussions that might appear to have a less debate-oriented goal, such as the charge to collectively summarize an author's argument, require students to reflect on differences among each of their interpretations of the reading. Thus, regardless of the goal of any particular discussion, students must have the opportunity to hear points of view that they hadn't considered before, and then try them on and give them a fair evaluation. This is why students have to listen carefully and respectfully to their peers and consider their various interpretations and opinions, as well as their justifications. Because the value of discussion lies in these transactions, it is also crucial that every student have a voice and express it. No wallflowers permitted. Remind your class about the purpose of discussion every few weeks.

A related approach is to ask students to articulate the elements of a good discussion and the qualities of a good discussion participant. Hollander (2002) poses these questions as a short, ungraded writing assignment and, on the day the assignment is due, leads a discussion on the factors that contribute to a good discussion. Invariably her students bring up factors that emphasize participants' behavior—that they prepare, express a variety of viewpoints, back up opinions with evidence or analysis, contribute fairly evenly, listen to each other, and respond respectfully. She reports that this strategy increases and helps equalize participation for the rest of the term.

Holding a brief discussion about discussion helps both to clarify its value and to reinforce the importance of preparation in order to get the most out of the learning experience. Helping students think metacognitively (McGuire, 2015) about the connection between discussion's purpose and process and its usefulness to their learning not only motivates students to prepare more effectively but also shows them how to participate in a discussion respectfully. Invite them to set some ground rules, suggesting as a guide how they want to be treated when they volunteer a possibly contentious contribution. The discussion that results will accustom them to hearing their own and their peers' voices and make it easier for them to speak up in subsequent classes. As the conventional wisdom goes, do on the first day of class whatever you want students to do throughout the term.

Third—and a clear way to reinforce your message about the key role that discussion will play in your course—is to include participation in the course grade. It does increase student preparation and participation (Dallimore, Hertenstein, & Platt, 2016) and even the participation of low-responding students (Williams et al., 2009). If you're an introvert, you may resist this idea. You may reflect back on the discomfort you felt speaking in any size class. But you did get over it, and you did so by being coaxed or perhaps pushed to speak. Participation grades need not penalize the less vocal student, though. You can deemphasize the *frequency* of contributions and include the completion of preparation assignments, the incorporation of outside sources into the dialogue, the ability to recognize and the willingness to challenge underlying assumptions, adherence to the discussion ground rules or format, and other factors related to the *quality* of the student's contributions. *How much* to count participation in the overall course grade inspires debate, and few faculty give it much weight—certainly not as much as they give exams and major assignments (Archer & Miller, 2011; Weimer, 2011). If discussion carries so much importance in a course, shouldn't we be counting it for more than 10% to 15% of the final grade?

If you decide to grade on participation, the next question is how, and it is not an easy task. You have to develop a new rubric or adapt an existing one. If you are teaching in a classroom, you have to keep track of something as ephemeral as speech. If you are teaching online, you have to assess a large amount of discussion forum text. However, you need not do all the assessing yourself. You can have students evaluate their own contributions, either all of them or their best ones, using a rubric or some criteria that you provide. You then respond to their self-evaluations or grades. For details about these methods, a long list of possible rubric criteria, and an example, go to the section "Assessing Individual Students' Contributions" in chapter 5.

Fourth, you can incentivize preparation and high-quality by rewarding them with recognition. After 15 to 20 minutes of discussion, ask students what they found to be the most insightful or useful contribution they heard in the past several minutes, or the one that brought more students into the discussion, or the one that offered the most helpful follow-up to ideas that another student volunteered (Bowen & Watson, 2017). This technique should accomplish the same purpose as grading participation but with less student and instructor effort.

Fifth, encourage students to prepare for discussion by assigning some kind of homework on the reading, video, or podcast that will serve as the basis for the discussion. Then you can either collect (electronically or in class) and award the homework some nominal value (in total, worth at least 20% of the final grade) or use it to justify cold-calling, preferably randomly, on any student without causing undue stress (Kastens, 2010). You can grade the participation or assume that peer pressure will motivate student preparation.

You can choose from many possible forms of homework. You can have students bring in two questions to ask, two quotations that best capture the thesis, or the most difficult point to understand in the assigned material (Cashin & McKnight, 1986). You can have them mark passages in the readings that are puzzling, novel, interesting, provocative, central, or related to other readings or discussion themes. Then ask students to read the passages aloud in class and explain why they selected these particular excerpts. This activity can launch a discussion in which each student in turn responds to his or her peers' choices and insights (Barkley, 2010). Alternatively, distribute study questions in advance on the assigned reading, video, or podcast that reflect those on which you will be basing the discussion. Then allow students to refer to their notes or written answers to the study questions during the discussion. Although this is a very old idea, scholars still mention it occasionally (e.g., Brooks, 2011). As suggested by participants in a 2016 POD Conference roundtable session (Herman & Nilson, 2016), you can, for example, furnish study or reflection questions in advance and have students write their answers as homework and bring them to class. They can share their answers in small groups and decide the best answers to report out. Yet another idea is to have students write a double journal of their thoughts as they read, view, or listen to the homework, with one side of the page reserved for their public thoughts and the other side their private ones.

As stated at the beginning of this section, inducing students to complete whatever homework you assign to prepare them for a discussion is a necessary although not sufficient condition for a fruitful exchange. Happily, you have your choice of many ways to build in accountability, motivation, and incentives—instituting compliance mechanisms, explaining the value of preparatory assignments and discussion itself, recognizing responsible students, grading on participation, and assigning meaningful written homework on the preparatory content.

Principle 2: Students Must Feel Safe to Express Themselves

When faculty discuss safety in the classroom, they typically mean emotional or psychological safety. The idea of safety as a necessary foundation for authentic, productive discussion has generated dialogue and research on "safe," "respectful," "free," and other types of spaces; the idea of safety versus comfort; microaggressions; trigger warnings; difficult conversations; and ground rules or course contracts for respectful interaction. Identities and the intersectionality of those identities, particularly in regard to historically marginalized groups, are often at the heart of this dialogue, as are concepts like implicit bias and privilege.

These concepts, issues, and debates all relate to the idea of *course climate*, or the "intellectual, social, emotional, and physical environments in which our students learn" (Ambrose, Bridges, DiPietro, Lovett, & Norman, 2010, p. 170). Research has shown that course climate impacts both motivation and learning (Pascarella & Terenzini, 1991). A number of factors contribute to course climate, including interactions between faculty and students and among students themselves, the tone set in the course, instances of stereotyping or tokenizing, classmate demographics, and course content (Ambrose et al., 2010). These factors influence whether the course climate may marginalize certain groups of students. In fact, DeSurra and Church (1994) found that most college classrooms have an "implicitly marginalizing" course climate (pp. 24–25)—that is, faculty unintentionally create a negative climate for at least some of the students. Ambrose and colleagues (2010) cite various studies that demonstrate the adverse impact of this negative climate on student learning (Hall, 1982; Hurtado, Milem, Clayton-Pedersen, & Allen, 1999; Watson, Terrell, & Wright, 2002; Whitt, Nora, Edison, Terenzini, & Pascarella, 1999) and urge faculty to proactively and explicitly create structures to generate a positive climate for all students.

How, then, can faculty create structures that lead to an encouraging course climate so that students feel safe expressing themselves in discussion? In chapter 3, we present strategies for handling sensitive subjects, trigger warnings, and microaggressions.

Principle 3: Students Need Good Reasons to Listen Actively

If you regularly ask students to react to each other's contributions, you're already giving them one good reason to listen actively to the discussion, especially if their participation affects their course grade. But you have other tools at your disposal as well.

Let's begin with actions you can take to make it easier for your students to pay attention. First, supply a broad discussion outline or road map that lists the learning objectives for the discussion, the topics, and/or the questions you will ask. This way, students are able to keep up with your organization. Second, write the major points made on the board. This technique honors students' contributions and facilitates their listening. Third, advise students on how to take notes on discussion, which includes telling them specifically *when* to take notes during the first few discussions. Students have enough trouble taking notes during a well-structured lecture. They leave out important material, such as examples of applications, descriptions of demonstrations, the structure of arguments, and instructor corrections, and they miscopy equations and graphics from the board (Johnstone & Su, 1994; Kiewra, 1985, 2005). So taking notes on a discussion, which zigzags among points and participants, may overwhelm them; in fact, it may never have occurred to them to take notes on such an apparently disjointed activity. Yet, if you have significant learning objectives for the exchange, students need to record the key arguments and the conclusions drawn. Tell them when they have reached a milestone worth writing down, or assign one student to do this in a small-group discussion. If the discussion has features of a debate, have students draw a line down the middle of the page to summarize the main points and rebuttals on each side of the issue.

Now let's turn to what you can do to motivate your students to listen actively. First, include discussion content in quizzes and exams and design assignments to require material from the discussions. These assignments may be journal entries, written case debriefings, papers, reports, projects, designs, works of art, or any other student-generated products. Second, if you break your class into small discussion groups, randomly call on a few to summarize their progress, conclusions, or answers, and randomly select the spokesperson within each group. To avoid your own biases, select the spokesperson on some playful criterion: the member of the group with the most recent birthday or the lightest color shirt or top, for example. Third, close a discussion by randomly selecting a student to summarize it and then solicit other students to add major points. Fourth, close a discussion by asking students to write a one-minute paper responding to one or more reflective prompts, such as the most important, valuable, or useful thing(s) they learned during the discussion; the most unexpected or surprising thing(s) they learned; or the material they found most confusing. It is best to collect these reflections so students complete them and to read a sample of them to learn how students experienced the discussion.

Principle 4: Students Respond Well to a Variety of Structured Discussion Formats

Faculty have successfully used a number of structured discussion formats in many course settings. Some of these formats help achieve a particular goal, such as brainstorming or debate; others help equalize student participation; and many can do both. Here we describe three kinds of structured formats that are designed to achieve a particular pedagogical goal and, in the next section, consider them as mechanisms to encourage more equal engagement.

The gallery walk is one type of structured discussion that facilitates brainstorming, exploring specific ideas in depth, or building constructively on previous responses. In this format, the professor places sheets of paper around the room, each with a different prompt. These prompts can include questions to answer, problems to solve, ideas to brainstorm, or concept maps to create. You begin by getting the students out of their seats and breaking them into small groups of typically four to five students and assigning each group to a different piece of paper. The groups then have a set period of time—perhaps three to five minutes—to generate ideas or solutions in response to the prompt and record their thoughts on the paper. You can ask students either to discuss and contribute individually (all students should have markers in their hands to do so) or to come to consensus and have one student record for the group, although the former approach tends to generate more ideas and dialogue. After the set period of time has passed, the groups then rotate to a new paper and prompt and repeat the process, generating new ideas and building on the ideas of the group that preceded them. After all the groups have visited each piece of paper, have a few "open walk" minutes in which students can review and comment on all of the responses. There are a number of effective variations on the gallery walk (Francek, 2006, 2016; Kolodner, 2004; Taylor, 2001), but they all give groups the opportunity to review, analyze, and contribute to the ideas of previous groups through iterative, short discussion sessions. This format helps students appreciate and build constructively on each other's ideas.

A second common structured discussion format is the debate. It can help students develop a deeper understanding of an argument or consider opposing viewpoints as well as improve their information literacy and critical thinking skills. When preparing for debate, ask students to review reputable sources that present each side and mine these sources for evidence to support one or both sides. You can structure the in-class discussion in one of several ways:

- change-your-mind debate, in which students assigned to each side develop and deliver an evidence-based, compelling argument (either on the side they select or the side opposed to their personal views) to sway a neutral group, which is charged with asking each side challenging questions; and

- simulation of a real-world process, such as a press conference or court proceeding, in which the students role-play various positions (judge, prosecuting and defense attorney, expert witnesses, jury, etc.).

The third format is the fishbowl discussion (Cummings, 2015; R.L. Miller & Benz, 2008; K.R. White, 1974; Zhang, 2013), in which a smaller group of students discusses a topic while a larger group quietly observes and takes notes on the content. Many faculty seat students in two concentric circles. The fishbowl requires the observing students to listen for understanding rather than focus on forming a response, which helps develop active listening skills. Typically, the groups switch positions partway through the discussion, and sometimes the second group is asked to summarize the previous group's ideas and explicitly reference or tie these ideas to new contributions. When structured this way, this format can help students build off each other's ideas rather than make siloed comments or just waiting for their turn to speak. Another version of the fishbowl is problem based, in which the central group is charged with solving a problem through discussion, and the outer group listens and acts as advisers when needed (Miller & Benz, 2008).

These are just a few examples of structured discussion formats among the many in publication. Some books provide an organized compilation of discussion formats with clear directions and applications for practice. For example, Brookfield and Preskill (2016) describe the commonly used jigsaw technique, a classic discussion structure that we describe later in this chapter. Other publications, such as Angelo and Cross's (1993) and Barkley, Major, and Cross's (2014) work, contain a variety of pedagogical techniques, some of which can be applied or adapted as a structured discussion format—focused listing (Angelo & Cross, 1993), for example—that facilitates brainstorming.

Principle 5: Students Contribute as Equally as the Discussion Structure Requires

Let's turn back to the gallery walk, debate, and fishbowl to see how they generate more equal engagement. In the gallery walk, students work in a small discussion group but build on classmates' comments individually, and others build off theirs. This format also gives introverts processing time so that they can contribute fully after having time to form their ideas. In the debate format, students have clear roles or tasks; the more specific the role or task (e.g., the courtroom scenario), the more that each student's contribution is essential and expected. Students are also doing plenty of preparation work ahead of time to ensure that they thoughtfully prepare their argument before class. Finally, in the fishbowl format, students alternate between active contribution and active listening. This format provides clear roles for each stage of the discussion and allows extroverts and introverts to practice less familiar discussion roles.

Faculty can use techniques other than structured formats to generate more equal participation in discussion. Listed here are suggestions from participants in the 2016 POD Conference roundtable session (Herman & Nilson, 2016) mentioned earlier. Some involve giving quieter students time to prepare answers or having dominating students participate as listeners:

- Ask students to write down their ideas before responding, or give them 10 to 15 seconds to reflect before allowing responses.
- Assign to each group an active listener charged with summarizing others' ideas back to the group.
- Ask students who haven't contributed yet to summarize another person's comments and build off those with a new idea.
- Give dominating students three pennies to track their comments to help them keep their tendency toward overparticipation in check (see chapter 3 for more detail on this technique).

Other suggestions involve structuring deliverables to involve all students:

- Provide the discussion questions before class, and ask students to type up answers as homework. During a small-group discussion, ask the group members to share their answers and then create a new set of "best answers" as a group.
- Assign students a specific number of concrete deliverables to formulate in a specific time frame. For example, each person has two minutes to come up with three examples of a concept, and then each group has an additional three minutes to discuss and select three examples to report to the class. Concrete deliverables help keep all members on task. This also works well in large classes, particularly if you use polling technology (such as Socrative or Poll Everywhere) to enable all groups to instantly share their results.

- Lead a brainstorm using the snowball or round-robin system. Keep a running list of students' ideas on a flipchart or whiteboard, where each student mentions an idea that hasn't been mentioned yet.
- Use a rotating student facilitator. During the last 10 minutes of class discussion, the facilitator leads a discussion of "What haven't we said yet?" (The facilitator can also help the class summarize key points from the discussion.)

Principle 6: Students Respond Well to Questions With Multiple Good Answers

Recitation questions ask students to reproduce or say in their own words content that they are supposed to have learned from listening to you or from completing the assigned readings or other homework. These questions have one correct answer, even if it can be phrased in different ways, so they do not reflect a point of view or require justifications. Recitation questions have their time and place, but a discussion is not one of them. In fact, students shy away from these questions because they are afraid of either getting the answer wrong or looking like an apple polisher (a student who is trying to gain special favor with the instructor) in front of the class when they give a correct answer.

In contrast, good discussion questions encourage participation because their answers are more complex or varied and move beyond simple recall. Most discussion questions have multiple correct answers, and all good discussion questions have multiple ways of phrasing or approaching these correct answers. Students know that if they are prepared and give a clear, thoughtful explanation, their odds of giving a respectable response are anywhere from pretty good to excellent. (They also understand that these questions have plenty of unacceptable answers.) They know that they can contribute even if other students spoke up first. Good discussion questions have another virtue, too: They demand higher level thinking. In Bloom's taxonomy (1956), this means application, analysis, synthesis, or evaluation.

Perhaps the best questions are *open-ended* ones (Brookfield & Preskill, 2005; Vella, 2008) because they invite creativity and a wide range of well-meaning responses. Brainstorming questions fit into this category. You can ask students to brainstorm examples, topics, problems, solutions to a problem, interpretations, possible consequences—almost anything. In classic brainstorming, participants put everything they can think of on the table—that is, record all the responses on the board, a slide, or a flipchart, if they are not already on a discussion forum—and evaluate the ideas later. Principle 4 in this chapter describes other examples of brainstorming strategies. Another option is to pose a question that is currently unresolved in your discipline. You might hear this type of query at the next conference you attend. Perhaps research has obtained contradictory results or even anomalies to the dominant paradigm, or scholars dispute how to proceed with the line of research. When you tell students that these questions represent genuine unknowns in your discipline, they will feel freer to speculate responses and will acquire a more sophisticated understanding of your field as subject to uncertainties and as a fluid, human endeavor versus the textbook depiction as a frozen aggregate of definitions, principles, and procedures. With this understanding, your students will begin to appreciate the true nature of knowledge.

Like open questions, *hypothetical questions* (Brookfield & Preskill, 2005) welcome creativity but in response to a what-if question. Students have to make up plausible ramifications or extrapolations to changing conditions or parameters by drawing on some combination of research, course content, and prior knowledge and experience. These questions can lead students to define the limits of a relationship or phenomenon. For instance, what would happen if college tuition were eliminated? If there were a major volcanic eruption in Yellowstone Park? If parents could choose the gender of their children?

Other types of questions are more reality bound. For example, you can have students describe a *cause-and-effect* relationship between facts, concepts, historical events, phenomena, and the like that goes beyond the course material (Brookfield & Preskill, 2005; McKeachie, 2002). Such questions can help students connect the course content to their own experiences, other disciplines, or research they could conduct themselves. *Comparative questions* (McKeachie, 2002) demand analysis of the similarities and differences between theories, literary works, research studies, phenomena, events, and so on. You can pose *critical* or *evaluative questions* (McKeachie, 2002) about the effectiveness of a given approach, procedure, solution, or recommendation or the validity of a particular argument, claim, research finding, or interpretation, including one that a classmate recently posited. You might ask students to select a position from several possibilities and justify their choice with evidence and logic. Alternatively, you can take a contentious, controversial stance on an issue and ask your students to argue for or against it.

Some of the answers that students provide to any type of question may seem unclear or embryonic. In this case, you can follow up with a *clarification question* or one *requesting more evidence* (Brookfield & Preskill, 2005). You might ask a student (in a matter-of-fact way) for a rephrasing, an elaboration, an application, an illustration, or a defense of the stated position. This defense may involve additional evidence, stronger evidence, or a rebuttal to a credible counterargument.

Finally, close a discussion with one or more *summary and synthesis tions* (Brookfield & Preskill, 2005), which ask students to reflect on the session and identify some types of points or ideas—perhaps the most important or the most surprising ones, ideas that the discussion clarified, or even points that remain puzzling or unresolved. Such questions induce students to review the discussion and make sense of it as a whole.

Principle 7: Students Benefit From Having Time to Think Before Contributing

When we ask a question, we can mistakenly expect a quick response. We may think that what we consider a long delay indicates that students didn't prepare or don't understand what you said or are quietly rejecting you. We may regard a period of silence as some kind of failure on our part. We may even back away from our question and ask another one, confusing students and possibly extending the delay. Then when one or two students put up their hand, we jump to call on them, lest the hush of crickets becomes deafening. These are almost always the same students—the fearless extroverts who have the faith to finish their sentences on the fly.

Most students, however, need up to 15 seconds or even longer to craft a response that they are comfortable sharing publicly, and they will be happy to hear you say that you will wait so many seconds before asking for responses. They need this time to process the question, retrieve the relevant content, and assemble an answer using the foreign language of the discipline. We are much too fluent in the disciplinary language and knowledge to appreciate the cognitive effort that our students—especially the not-so-fearless introverts, English language learners, and students with learning and other disabilities—give to formulating a decent response. The additional time may also help extroverted students, who are inclined to begin speaking immediately, to more carefully consider what ideas they want to convey. Even waiting just a few seconds can dramatically increase the proportion of students with an answer ready and the quality of those answers. More students means broader participation, especially among the more reserved ones, so you need not rely on the few who typically dominate. In fact, you need not rely on raised hands: You can look for nonverbal signs of readiness to speak, such as eye contact or an open facial expression. You can also cold-call on students who have not participated in a while. If you prefer to call on students randomly, you can use a name randomizer on a computer or simply shuffle index cards with student names and pick a card from the top of the deck.

Be careful with cold-calling, however, as some students may be incapable of showing what they know under pressure. You may be able to identify them because they probably haven't spoken in class at all. They may be dealing with emotional, social, cultural, language, or medical issues that explain their lack of voluntary participation (see the later section entitled "Challenge 4: Perpetually Silent Students" in chapter 3). Such students benefit from special advance preparation for class. Speak to them personally and provide them with at least some of the discussion prompts you are planning. You might want to give them one or two questions in particular that you'd like them to answer during the next class and have them rehearse their response with you.

Perhaps you have presented a task or a question that you expect students to find particularly challenging or complex. It may be a novel case to debrief, a paradox to resolve, a problem that requires the integration of lessons, or something else that requires students to think critically or creatively. Or perhaps you just have a reticent class. Your students may need more than several more seconds to think. You can ask them to outline or write out their answer first. Or, you can use those 30 seconds or so to think about or write about the question or task on their own and then break them into pairs or small groups to write down a response within a minute or two. (If you use groups, walk around the room to make sure they stay on task.) Either of these tactics will help students muster their confidence and will probably yield more and better quality responses.

You needn't wait for volunteers to answer: You can preempt the discussion and let the students know that you will ask individuals, pairs, or groups to share their responses. Overall, students will feel more prepared to answer (and more motivated to generate quality ideas) because they can read what's in front of them. You can also ask pairs or groups to select a spokesperson to share the best ideas of the group so that all students are contributing, even if only one person from the group is speaking.

Technology can also buy students the time that they need. If you are teaching a face-to-face class, you can move the question or task to an online discussion board and take advantage of the generous thinking time that asynchronous learning affords. In class, you can break the ice by polling the students with a personal response system on their initial reactions to the question or task (Bali & Greenlaw, 2016), and then have them discuss the question in small groups before either polling again as a group or discussing the question overall as a class.

Principle 8: Students Can Benefit From Expressing Themselves in Motion and Space

Deliberately integrating physical spaces and movement into discussion design can benefit student learning by enhancing motivation and morale, strengthening learning and memory (Doyle & Zakrajsek, 2013), and actively including and involving all students in the class. When students are out of their seats and moving, they can't be disengaged in the back row. In addition, the novelty of these techniques can help increase student interest and motivation.

Motion-and-space discussion strategies can serve several purposes: brainstorming, illustrating and engaging students with varying perspectives, illustrating a concept, and adding structure to or reinforcing deliverables. First, brainstorming exercises include chalk talks (Smith, 2009), in which students brainstorm in large groups at the whiteboard; gallery walks, which we explained previously; and "rotating stations" (Brookfield & Preskill, 2016, pp. 43–47), which is another version of the gallery walk.

Second, strategies for illustrating or engaging students with varying perspectives include an exercise in which each corner of the room represents a different perspective or topic for discussion, and students either self-select or are assigned to one of the corners to discuss the topic. Brookfield and Preskill (2016) describe a version of this exercise called "Stand Where You Stand" (pp. 135–138), which focuses on the corners representing degrees of agreement with an issue. You can also use each corner to represent a different theoretical perspective or analytical lens and have students discuss an idea using that lens when physically located in that corner. The folding line exercise also uses space to illustrate multiple perspectives (Herman & Nilson, 2016): Students arrange themselves in a line according to where their position on a question, debate, or controversial issue falls on a continuum. When the line "folds," students on one extreme of the line are placed into a group with students from the other end, and they then discuss or debate the issue. Alternatively, students can argue the other side's perspective and/or the extreme discussion groups can try to persuade the middle group.

Third, some movement-based activities illustrate a complex concept, often through simulation or role-play, and can launch a discussion on the topic immediately following the experience. These discussions comprise debriefing the experience itself (what happened, feelings or reactions, results, etc.) as well as connecting the experience to the underlying concept that it was designed to illustrate. Examples of such experiences include the privilege walk (McIntosh, 1989) and intercultural communication simulations, such as BáFá BáFá (Shirts, 1977), among other such cross-disciplinary exercises.

Fourth, movement and space can add structure or reinforce deliverables in a discussion. For some examples, ask students to record their group's ideas on flipchart paper and post it to the wall, or write their ideas on sticky notes to post on a brainstorming wall, or move to a different seating arrangement to report out results. Jigsaw discussions (Brookfield & Preskill, 2016) also use physical movement as structure: Students discuss a topic in small groups with the goal of becoming "experts" on that topic. Then the students move into new small groups, each with one representative of each of the previous groups. These experts then teach their specialty to the new group. The physical movement from one group to the next reinforces the change in task and discussion topic.

Principle 9: Students Can Benefit From Expressing Themselves Graphically

Allow individual students, pairs, and small groups to draw their answers when appropriate. With their responses expressed on paper or a screen in front of them, they should feel relatively at ease explaining their graphic and the thinking behind it to the class.

Students will probably need your guidance on the most suitable type of graphic to use. A sequence of events or operations, or causal or procedural process, calls for a flowchart. So you might ask students to draw a flowchart of the managerial decision-making process, the best way to conduct an epidemiological research study, or a strategy to approach a problem-based learning assignment. By contrast, hierarchically organized concepts, categories, equations, topics, or principles are best shown in a concept map or mind map. So you might recommend that students use a concept or mind map to respond to your queries about the organization of the federal executive branch, the relationships among animals in a phylum, or the earth as a geological system.

Concept circle diagrams, such as a Venn diagram, can illustrate all kinds of relationships among concepts, categories, equations, topics, or principles, especially when they overlap in some way (Wandersee, 2002). Using these diagrams, students can answer your questions about the degree of difference and similarity between related entities, such as deviance and lawbreaking (partially overlapping), tort and contract law (separate, no overlapping), and capital budgeting and sensitivity analysis (the former encompassing the latter). A mathematics professor used circle concept diagrams to summarize the complex relationships among explicit, first-order, ordinary differential equations, some of which overlap and others of which encompass another (Nilson, 2016). He could have purposely made errors in his diagram for students to identify during a discussion.

Matrices accommodate comparisons and contrasts among different events, processes, concepts, principles, and the like—such as types of literature, different chemical bonds, twentieth-century wars involving the United States, and categories of astronomical objects—as well as ways to classify them. Therefore, they are excellent tools to use during a wrap-up or review discussion. Students set them up by putting the entities for comparison and contrast down the far left column and the comparison and contrast criteria across the top. Then they fill in the cells. They can do this in a small-group or in a whole-class discussion, face-to-face or online. To challenge students more, you can have them come up with the comparison and contrast criteria.

Research tells us that students benefit in several ways when you give them the opportunity to represent their learning of the material graphically.

First, developing a graphic requires students to think conceptually. Whatever the graphic, concepts form the building blocks, and the arrangements of these blocks symbolize and illustrate the relationships among them. The relationships are best specified with labels.

Second, a graphic conveys the concepts and their interrelationships more efficiently than does text. In technical terms, it carries a lower cognitive load, demanding less working memory and fewer cognitive transformations than text (Larkin & Simon, 1987; Mayer, 2005, 2009; Mayer & Moreno, 2003; D.H. Robinson, Katayama, DuBois, & Devaney, 1998; D.H. Robinson & Kiewra, 1995; D.H. Robinson & Molina, 2002; D.H. Robinson & Schraw, 1994; D.H. Robinson & Skinner, 1996). Text presents information sequentially one piece at a time, and the mind must put these pieces together, often interpreting and prioritizing them, then reassembling them. A graphic, by contrast, displays the information holistically, showing both the individual components and the relationships among them at the same time. The shapes of enclosures, the colors, the connection labels, and other visual elements may also convey information. The lighter load that graphics place on the mind leaves more mental resources available for *thinking* about the material, so students can more easily apply, analyze, extract, and draw inferences about it (Larkin & Simon, 1987; Vekiri, 2002).

Third, graphics depend less on words and thus offer another advantage: They communicate across cultures and levels of language facility. Many of the conventions they follow, such as the use of arrows to show movement or direction and spatial proximity to indicate how closely components are related, seem to be universal and apparently reflect basic human processes of visual perception (Tversky, 1995, 2001).

Finally, graphics facilitate the processing, storage, and retrieval of knowledge. Constructivism posits that students learn by constructing knowledge (Vygotsky, 1978), not memorizing it, and drawing graphics requires them to organize material on their own. Whatever the type of graphic, it furnishes a ready-made structure on which students can map or recast knowledge. It helps students, who are novices in our field, see the big picture of the patterns, generalizations, and abstractions that experts recognize so clearly, as well as the central concepts and principles. The mind relies on this structured big picture to process, store, and retrieve knowledge. In processing and storage, the mind integrates new material not into a collection of facts and terms but into a coherent, preexisting organization of prior knowledge (Bransford, Brown, & Cocking, 1999; Hanson, 2006; Svinicki, 2004; Wieman, 2007). In retrieval, the mind can easily recall the shape of the graphic because the shape moves effortlessly from the working memory into the long-term memory, and this visual-spatial memory trace then cues the text (Richard Pak, personal correspondence May 13 and December 12, 2013). You may have had the college experience of recalling text-based content, perhaps during a test, by remembering the layout of the page of the book where you read it.

Dual-coding theory also offers an explanation as to why graphics help students store and retrieve material. It proposes that our mind has two memories, the semantic and the episodic, corresponding to the verbal and visual-spatial systems, respectively (Paivio, 1971). The theory has recently gained new credibility, as neuroscience and cognitive psychological research has provided evidence that the human mind processes and stores verbal and visual-spatial information in separate cognitive systems (Vekiri, 2002). When creating or even just studying a graphic, students process and store the material in both systems, not only in the verbal system that processes text and spoken words (Moreno & Mayer, 1999). In fact, the mind retains any knowledge that it receives in multiple modes (e.g., visual, verbal, auditory, and kinesthetic) better and longer—and retrieves it more easily—than knowledge processed through only one channel (Kosslyn, 1994; Mayer, 2005, 2009; Mayer & Moreno, 2003; Mayer & Sims, 1994; Paivio, 1971, 1990; Paivio & Csapo, 1973; Paivio, Walsh, & Bons, 1994; Svinicki, 2004; Tigner, 1999; Tulving, 1985; Vekiri, 2002).

Principle 10: Students Respond Well to Novel Stimuli, Such as Outside Ideas or Research

Kolb's experiential learning cycle explains that students learn best when they engage in a cycle of having a concrete experience, then reflecting and learning from that experience, and finally applying their understanding to a new experience (Kolb, 1984). Introducing new knowledge, content, theories, or models during this process promotes learning. Discussion can provide a structure for integrating outside ideas or research into the learning process. Here, we explain ways that you can introduce content in preparation for discussion, during discussion, or as part of an iterative or ongoing discussion.

Having students review outside information in preparation for discussion may be the most common approach to incorporating content. This can involve assigning a reading or video or having the students find and read an article or a website as homework. It can also include in-class content delivery, such as lecture before discussion. One interesting strategy relies on the jigsaw approach, in which each member of a small discussion group completes a different reading for class, and the discussion begins by having each student share a summary, key points, and analysis of his or her assigned reading with the group; the task is then to discuss a question or issue that is informed by these readings. You may also assign articles that provide different perspectives—or even conflicting ones—on the topic at hand. This approach enriches discussion by asking students to incorporate and reference outside perspectives and provides excellent preparation for debate.

You can also draw on students' out-of-class experiences as preparation for discussion. In this method, students analyze how a recent experience—such as service-learning, lab, simulation, interviews, field observation, or any other hands-on activity—aligns with or deviates from the findings in the literature or how a particular theory explains it. You can have students make these connections in writing before class and then summarize, share, analyze, and compare their reflections with their group.

You can introduce outside ideas or research during discussion as well. In a webquest, for instance, students seek out information, examples, or ideas online to answer a question or explain a complex concept. For example, in her Non-Formal Education course, Herman asked her students to find a cartoon and quotation online that they thought best summarized Paulo Freire's critique of traditional education systems and explain how their finds illustrated his ideas (Friere, 1970). You can also give groups a list of sources such as websites, videos, or short online articles to research and discuss their answers to prepared questions. Consider furnishing each group with different resources to develop their responses.

If you teach lecture-oriented or content-heavy courses, you can also interweave lecture and discussion, which breaks up the lecture, reduces cognitive load, and enriches discussion with new content. We've seen faculty in both chemistry and finance apply this interactive lecture format around *pinch points*, which are concepts that students find particularly challenging. In a pinch point interactive lecture, you lecture for 10 to 15 minutes and then ask students to discuss the content for 2 to 3 minutes—that is, share their understanding of the new concepts in pairs or small groups, clarify how this content fits into the organization of the lecture, and generate questions for you. After answering these questions, you move to the next part of the lecture, repeating this iterative process. In addition, you can have students review text or video content online before class and discuss their questions in groups at the beginning of class. Each group then asks you any remaining questions, which in turn guide your lecture. According to faculty who have tried this approach, the pinch points tend to be predictable, so you can prepare your lectures ahead of time. Because you focus only on the pinch points, you can typically cover more content, and the discussion format increases student engagement and retention of the material.

Iterative or ongoing discussion follows a model in which each discussion builds on the one from the previous class, and students develop an increasingly complex understanding of a concept as more and more data accumulate. For example, students might read articles or hear a lecture and then summarize a debate. For the next class, they might be tasked with gathering external evidence to support a side in the debate and then discuss again in the next class.

Following Kolb's cycle, another approach is to use discussion to help students analyze how new content informs their understanding and use of an experiential piece. This works well in courses that focus on skill development or benefit from scaffolding, such as statistical analysis or writing.

Finally, you can infuse content into recurring discussion in a team-based, project-based learning format where you provide content and consulting advice to the teams. We have seen this model in courses ranging from grant writing to finance investment, with particular success in competition-based courses. Each class session features a small-group discussion based around the new content and its implications for or application to the project.

Principle 11: Students Participate According to How Effectively a Discussion Is Moderated

We often use the phrase "leading a discussion" to describe our desired role in the exchange. But the verb *leading* may put us on a somewhat too dominant plane because we really want our students to take over and maintain the flow of the dialogue. The verbs *moderating* or *facilitating* might be more helpful descriptors of our role in the discussion. As a moderator or facilitator, we need to keep the spotlight on the students. In whatever we do or say, we should encourage them to think and talk.

Therefore, before commenting on a student contribution, ask other students for their reactions or invite them to build on it. "What do you think of that comment?" "How might you qualify that broad claim?" "Do you agree or disagree with that interpretation, and why?" "Can you think of any other reasons (examples, factors, evidence, causes, etc.) to add?" "Who can rephrase that point to make sense to someone who has never had a course on _____?" In some cases, you might ask students to address their remarks directly to each other rather than through you. You can open up the floor to multiple contributions by specifying that you'd like a certain number of responses to a given question—perhaps three to five different answers. If your students are splitting into camps on an issue, recast the discussion into a spontaneous debate. Let uncommitted or unsure students stand on the side of the room representing their current leanings and switch sides of the room if their mind changes during or after the debate. For a challenging twist, have each side argue in favor of the opposite position. At the point when you feel like an unnecessary party in the room or forum, you have achieved the height of success.

However, sometimes a moderator must step in. If no student provides the needed additions, clarification, or critique; or if a student gives faulty information; or if the discussion wanders off track, you might have to supply what's missing, furnish correct information, or refocus the exchange. If the discussion becomes heated or offensive to some students, you should also intervene. For ways to do this most effectively, go to chapter 3, "Preventing and Responding to Common Discussion Pitfalls," specifically the section entitled "Microaggressions" (p. 46). This section also addresses ways to set the stage for discussing potentially hot-button and controversial topics.

Finally, before moving on to another topic, you should inquire if anyone has something to add or qualify and then close by asking a student to summarize the main points made during the discussion.

Principle 12: Students Must See Their Personal Value as Separate From the Value of Their Contributions

Sometimes students have difficulty perceiving discussion as part of the learning process and instead view it as a form of presentation or evaluation. They come into the classroom thinking that it might reveal whether or not they understand the material, or are even prepared in the first place, which quickly devolves into fears of being seen as stupid or inadequate in some way. These students are conflating their self-worth with the quality of their contributions. Their mind-set can exacerbate this problem: Students with a fixed mind-set tend to view their intelligence and abilities as immutable (Dweck, 2016); therefore, less-than-stellar contributions in a class discussion become judgments on their character and overall worth as a human being rather than just a step in the learning process. This phenomenon may also lead students to "tell the professors what they want to hear"—in other words, what the student perceives as the correct answer—rather than being authentically engaged in wrestling with the content being discussed.

Ideally, faculty can help students separate their sense of self-worth from their take on how others view their performance in class discussion. For instance, you can verbally frame the purpose or importance of the discussion as a form of practice (with feedback) that will help them prepare for later evaluation in a paper or on an exam. This explanation shifts students' anxiety and self-judging out of the discussion and gives them permission to make mistakes; it's a trial run, after all. You can also frame the discussion as skills that they are developing, but be explicit: Explain exactly what skills, such as the ability to summarize and select important points from a source or the ability to listen to and understand another person's argument. Follow up with what students can do to improve these skills, such as preparing for class with key points from the text. This also drives home the point that success derives from work and preparation. Another way to frame discussion is as a tool to help develop a deeper understanding of the content. You might explain Bloom's taxonomy (Anderson & Krathwohl, 2001; Bloom, 1956) and how discussion helps students move beyond memorization to analysis or synthesis.

In addition to verbally framing the purpose of discussion, you can structure it to detach the response from the individual contributor in one of two ways. First, you can use techniques where students share *someone else's* ideas on difficult or controversial issues. In the card swap, students write a question or a response on a 3-inch-by-5-inch card without writing their names; you then ask the students to stand and continuously swap cards for about 30 seconds to ensure that no one knows the origin of the individual card. Students then use the question or comment on their new card to contribute to the discussion. In the similar snowball exercise, students write a question or response on a piece of paper, crumple it up, toss it across the room (like snowballs), retrieve someone else's crumpled paper, and use the ideas on it in the discussion.

Second, you can have students contribute their ideas anonymously to ensure their honesty while sparking conversation. Classroom response systems (clickers) and web- or app-based polling tools, such as Poll Everywhere or Socrative, can help you quickly gather class-wide anonymous responses. Some classroom assessment techniques, such as the muddiest point or minute paper (Angelo & Cross, 1993), can be anonymized. You can also use anonymous entrance or exit slips or online surveys such as SurveyMonkey to gather class-wide feedback before or after class. These strategies may not help students move into a growth mind-set, but separating the response from the individual contributor helps minimize students' anxiety, self-criticism, and fear of judgment from others.

Conclusion

When engaging students in a discussion, you face challenges, but research has helped make the task easier. The 12 principles to guide class discussion are based on much of this research, so following them should increase the appeal of the material to students and give them the confidence to participate. We have furnished a wide range of options from which you can choose in managing discussions so you can select the ones that best fit your personal style and types of students.

Still, the 12 principles cannot guarantee that all your discussion sessions will engage all your students. Human individuals and groups are too complicated and varied not to present challenges. Fortunately, we can identify the most common challenges and draw on research to prevent and remedy them. Chapter 3 describes these challenges and provides evidence-based strategies and recommendations for addressing them.

3

PREVENTING AND RESPONDING TO COMMON DISCUSSION PITFALLS

Jennifer H. Herman and Linda B. Nilson

No matter how well you honor the 12 principles in chapter 2, discussions can still present challenges and go awry. We will describe what these challenges are, how they undermine student engagement and learning, how to prevent them from materializing, and how to intervene when they occur. Where appropriate, we will anchor our solutions in the 12 principles. The challenges that we will address are the following:

1. Students who dominate conversation
2. Crickets
3. Narcissists
4. Perpetually silent students
5. Students having a lack of opportunity to engage
6. Inattention and multitaskers
7. Personal attacks and related incivilities
8. Sensitive subjects and trigger warnings
9. Microaggressions
10. Students with autism spectrum disorder
11. Asynchronous online discussions
12. Synchronous online discussions

Challenge 1: Students Who Dominate Conversation

Students who take over class participation reinforce the default participation norms of most students, which are civil (but not active) attention and consolidation of responsibility in the vocal few (Howard, 2015; Karp & Yoels, 1976).

In other words, dominators narrow participation and make active listening unnecessary for most students. As a result, only a few of the potential viewpoints, opinions, and perspectives reach the table. Once this pattern becomes routinized, it's difficult to reverse, so it's crucial to intervene quickly.

You can start by explicitly setting the norm of broad participation, but you have to back this up with action. Institute (and enforce) a rule that any student who contributes cannot speak again until at least three other students have spoken (Brooks, 2011). Alternatively, use the "three-penny rule" that a student can make just three contributions during any given discussion (Herman & Nilson, 2016); students can use pennies or other small objects as a physical reminder or tool to track their number of contributions. After posing a question to the class, say that you will give students at least 10 or more seconds to think about the question before you call on anyone, and then do so. As Principle 7 explains in chapter 2, most students need more time to think than we typically give them. After an extended wait time, you should have many more prepared students from which to choose.

Sometimes dominators will hog the floor with well-meaning questions, but usually those questions are of little interest to the class as a whole. In this case, ask the students to discuss the issue with you after class. Sometimes dominators are not quite sure what's confusing them, so they will begin to ramble, believing they will talk their way to the point. You can seize the opportunity to interrupt them, distill what you think they are getting at, supply a quick answer, and move on. Alternatively, you can ask them to better define their question and raise it outside of class.

Other dominators want to answer every question so you'll perceive them as smart, well prepared for class, and on your side. Some of these students may also crave attention (McKeachie & Svinicki, 2014). Others may not pick up on social cues that they are talking too much (Gooblar, 2015), or they may come from cultures that value a dominating speaking style (Eberly Center for Teaching Excellence, Carnegie-Mellon University, 2008). A few may be struggling with autism spectrum disorder (see the subsection later on these students). You might want to speak to such students privately, letting them know that you appreciate their contributions in class but want to give other students the chance to show what they know or need help understanding (Eberly Center for Teaching Excellence, Carnegie-Mellon University, 2008; Gooblar, 2015; McKeachie & Svinicki, 2014).

Challenge 2: Crickets

This section begins with tips for helping some students speak at the beginning of class, thereby setting the norm for their peers. Next, we will discuss the strategies suggested in our contributed chapters.

At the beginning of any class, discussion focused or not, it is always a good idea to display an outline, an agenda, or a list of learning objectives. This turns student attention to the upcoming topics and activities and implies that you have an organized plan for the period. It also helps to get students on the same page.

Here are examples of a few other opening activities that serve this same purpose and offer students a low-risk opportunity to speak up:

- Ask students to summarize the last class.
- Ask them about the purpose of an event that happened during the last class, such as a demonstration, role play, video, or debate.
- Ask them several easy recall questions on the assigned readings or other homework.
- Ask them about how they reacted emotionally to the assigned readings or other homework.
- Give them a writing prompt, such as a reflective question, on the assigned readings or other homework.
- Ask them to brainstorm what they already know about a topic or what outcomes they expect of an experiment or a situation.

If discussion sags in the middle of class, one of the following activities should inspire students to contribute:

- Give students time to write down their answers before calling on anyone.
- Have one or more students read key text passages aloud. Then ask why these are key passages.
- Pose a controversial question or play devil's advocate, which means arguing in favor of an unpopular stance or opposing a position, to encourage some students to argue against it.
- Have them reflect on and write their reaction to a provocative statement.
- Break the class into groups and ask them to answer questions.
- Allow students to engage in conversation before responding.

Of course, the authors of our contributed chapters offer more elaborate strategies to engage students in discussion, and we highlight these examples in the next few paragraphs. Please refer to the chapters themselves for more detail.

In her face-to-face history course, Festle (chapter 6) uses *deliberative dialogue* in which students systematically share and listen to different ideas and points of view and then consider and evaluate the various sides. In preparation, students complete written homework in which they analyze and appraise the positions offered in the readings. This homework readies them to articulate and possibly revise their own stance on the issue by the end of the discussion.

In their online social work staff development course, Marquart and Drury (chapter 7) lead synchronous class discussions via typed chat and webcam. They both model productive dialogue by coteaching the class and provide their students with abundant feedback and encouragement using a participation grading rubric. In addition, they poll their students to identify their key takeaways at the end of each class and try to meet personally, at least once, with as many of their students as possible.

To prompt more participation from introverts, who are often a source of crickets, in her face-to-face leadership class, Shapiro (chapter 8) incorporates several innovative strategies in collaborative autoethnography (CAE). Following a six-stage process focused around student-generated reflective prompts, students act as researchers using their personal stories as data and analyze their stories in their broader social and relational context. As it turns out, these introverts have a lot to say.

In the previous bulleted list, we suggested giving students a reflective writing prompt to evoke discussion. Shewmaker (chapter 9) takes this further by marrying mindfulness with the contemplative pedagogy of informal writing, 7 to 10 minutes of it, in response to a complex prompt at the beginning of every class. She applies the idea of mindfulness to "being fully present with the course material" and finds that it generates stimulating, content-rich exchanges (p. 102).

Rather than breaking the ice with his students, Strean (chapter 10) starts his physical education courses in warm waters by minimizing the status distance and displaying hospitality, personal interest, and social connectedness. He, too, gives students time to chat with others and write about their responses before offering a contribution publicly.

Science labs are known for being dull occasions that students try to cut short, but not Townsend's (chapter 11) microbiology lab. Since she transformed her labs into authentic research experiences for her health-career-bound students, she fields more lab-group and full-class discussion, and just pure excitement, than she ever had before.

After breeding virtual crickets, Voegele (chapter 12) has reinvigorated the online discussions in her blended graduate-level education course by grounding the discussions in her students' field projects on curriculum, incentivizing active listening, and weaving the online with the classroom discussions.

Finally, Wilson (chapter 13) builds lively exchanges into his online chemistry course by basing them on students' independent research on a topic of career interest to them, complementary and alternative medicines (CAMs). Along with learning about CAMs, his students develop skills in critical thinking, especially in evaluating the credibility of scholarly journals and their articles.

Two other related discussion strategies merit mention because they work very effectively, and they both rely on "paying" students to contribute to a discussion. The first strategy pays out "participation money" (Chylinski, 2010, p. 25) and the instructor decides how much a given comment is worth and why, teaching students what constitutes high-quality and lower quality participation. In an experimental study, these discussion dollars inspired both more frequent and more equal participation (Chylinski, 2010).

The second strategy involves real money. Call it controversial or bribery, but it has helped students overcome their fear of failure; conquer their reticence; and, for some, develop intrinsic interest in the material. Lewes, a professor of English and women's and gender studies at Lycoming College, starts her face-to-face literature course by rewarding good-faith contributions to discussion with quarters. After a few classes, she begins rewarding only the first contribution during a class to encourage the quieter students to speak up while discouraging the dominators. Soon she selectively rewards only the better comments, which teaches students to discriminate quality and motivates them to give deeper responses. Then she eliminates the quarters and keeps a $10 bill in reserve for a "special occasion," as when a particularly shy student shares an astute insight (Lewes & Stiklus, 2007).

Challenge 3: Narcissists

Narcissists in discussion are easy to spot: They are the students who relate everything back to themselves. Like dominators, they may overcontribute, but the primary way that they create problems is by inappropriately and repeatedly stepping away from the content and focusing on personal experience. While students do learn better by relating new content to past experiences (Knowles, 1984), narcissists rarely focus on understanding concepts; rather, they treat discussion as a social rather than learning interaction, crave attention (McKeachie & Svinicki, 2014), or lack the ability—whether from shaky understanding or inexperience with the method—to meaningfully engage with the content.

When this type of student is treating discussion as a social or ego-boosting event rather than a learning experience, try adding more structure, such as framing the purpose of the discussion, giving clear directions that require students to tie personal experiences back to the content, asking for deliverables (e.g., a summary or an analysis) at the end to keep them on task, using one of the structured formats that we described earlier, or simply asking the students to avoid sharing personal experiences. Do address this issue quickly, before the "socialization" of in-class discussion becomes a class norm.

However, don't assume that all narcissistic students are attention seeking or not trying. Some of them don't know how to discuss content without telling a personal story, or perhaps they don't understand the material. You can ask students to turn in summaries, outlines, or questions from the reading before discussion; give a quiz so that students can check for understanding; or open with questions that focus on understanding. Some students also benefit from modeling (Bandura, 1986), so you might invite colleagues to your class to model an academic discussion early in the term. This demonstration sets expectations for engagement, which you can reference later when redirecting off-topic students.

Challenge 4: Perpetually Silent Students

Crickets refers to utter silence across an entire class, but the problem we're addressing here pertains to individual students who never talk or post. The possible reasons for silence are numerous. Students may be shy, reserved, or introverted; they may be dealing with a learning disability, anxiety, grief, depression, medical challenges, or autism (see the later section on students with autism spectrum disorder); the classroom climate may make them feel isolated or uneasy; their jobs may leave them perpetually exhausted; they may feel uncomfortable expressing themselves in English; they may come from a culture that frowns on students who speak out publicly; or there may be other reasons. Some of the remedies for crickets, specifically those remedies that reduce the risk of contributing, may bring out some of the ever-quiet students (Bold, 2001; Nilson, 2016):

- Ask the class several easy recall questions on the assigned readings or other homework. These questions will reduce anxiety, and after one or two students break the ice, others are more likely to feel comfortable speaking.
- Ask for students' emotional reactions to the assigned readings or other homework. Again, these are easy questions that should evoke a student reaction.
- Give a writing prompt, such as a reflective question, on the assigned readings or other homework. This exercise will refresh students' memory of the homework.

- Give students time to write down their answers before calling on anyone. They are more likely to contribute if they have their responses in front of them.
- Ask students to brainstorm what they already know about a topic or what outcomes they expect of an experiment or a situation. Because these questions have no wrong answers, they are low risk.
- Have one or more students read key text passages aloud, and then ask why these are key passages. Reticent students are more likely to speak after hearing themselves and their peers speak.
- Break the class into groups and ask them to answer questions. The answers may improve, and students are not taking on any individual risk.
- Allow students to engage in conversation before responding. This method can evoke contributions for the same reason as the immediately preceding bullet.
- Direct some questions, preferably those not requiring a lengthy response, to individual students or sectors of the room that have been quiet during the class. This technique ensures that you make eye contact with these students and lets them know that you haven't overlooked them.
- Rotate the role of closing facilitator among your students (Herman & Nilson, 2016). This individual independently leads the last 10 minutes of discussion on the topic of "What haven't we said yet?" All students will have the chance to speak sooner or later.
- Ask quiet students to visit you during office hours and ask them why they haven't participated recently. Perhaps they are facing one or more of the challenges listed at the beginning of this section. In any case, encourage them to participate. Whatever may be holding students back, give them a discussion prompt you'd like them to respond to during the next class and have them rehearse their answer with you.
- Extend students' participation by having them post to a class blog, wiki, discussion board, or chat. Sometimes students who are quiet in class can be surprisingly vocal in online discussion.

Challenge 5: Students Having a Lack of Opportunity to Engage

Classmates dominating conversation, narcissists, or structural challenges in the course, such as a large class size, can reduce the opportunities of some students to participate. Several of the discussion structures and strategies mentioned earlier, such as the gallery walk, the three-inch-by-five-inch card swap, and fishbowl, involve all students in dialogue; see Principle 4 and Principle 5 for more ideas. You can also use smaller groups as the primary discussion units, reporting out or debriefing afterward to the entire class, or as a warm-up to generate ideas for large class discussion. Many of these techniques and small-group formats work well in both large and small classes, and many encourage the participation of students who might not feel comfortable speaking up in a large group setting. You needn't worry that every group reporting out in a large class would be tedious and time-consuming because the sharing can take several more efficient forms: posting ideas on a discussion board, sharing visually on big pieces of paper or the whiteboard, switching key points with another group and responding, completing a group minute paper, or having only a few randomly selected groups report out (Herman & Nilson, 2016).

Challenge 6: Inattention and Multitaskers

You'll recognize inattentive students because they'll ask you questions you've already answered, answer a discussion question you didn't ask, or repeat a comment previously made by another student. Both your time and the class's time are too precious for repetition or irrelevancy.

- Say that you already answered the question and will repeat the answer only outside class or refer the inattentive student to other students. In advance, establish the norm of students referring their questions to at least three classmates or other sources before you answer a question (Millis & Cottell, 1998).
- Tell the inattentive student that the response just given doesn't answer the question you asked. Then ask the student to repeat what you did ask.
- When an inattentive student repeats a contribution already given by another student, gently say to the latter student, "You said something very much like this a few minutes ago, didn't you?"

Inattention is often but not always a result of so-called multitasking between class activities and the Internet. Despite student claims to the contrary, multitasking doesn't exist. The brain cannot perform two tasks unless they rely on different parts of the brain, as do talking and walking (Wickens, 2002, 2008). Talking involves the verbal and, in a conversation, the auditory mental channels, which operate independently of the psychomotor channel. Even then, learning to perform a psychomotor task can place demands on the visual, central processing (cognitive), and perhaps other resources as well. Actively listening to a discussion and doing almost anything on a cell phone or laptop use the same mental resources—at the very least, the verbal, the auditory, the central processing, and the visual. Therefore, students cannot follow a discussion and engage with the Internet simultaneously. In fact, learning complex new material consumes just about all of the visual, auditory, verbal, and central processing resources the mind has (Wickens, 2002, 2008). Students' attempts to multitask really involve task rotation or task switching, which results in more errors and requires more time than focusing on one task at one time (Crenshaw, 2008; Ophir, Nass, & Wagner, 2009).

You can explain this to your students, but your class may not take priority over their Internet activities. Some college students seem to be addicted to their cell phones, especially for "staying connected." In fact, 90% to 92% of them say that they use their cell phones in class for nonclass purposes, such as texting, tweeting, playing games, checking Facebook, and web surfing (McCoy, 2013; Tindell & Bohlander, 2012). Dozens of studies, many of which involve hundreds of students, document that this behavior reduces their learning, focus, academic engagement, and grades (e.g., Clayson & Haley, 2013; Duncan, Hoekstra, & Wilcox, 2012; Foerde, Knowlton, & Poldrack, 2006; Junco, 2012a, 2012b, 2012c; Junco & Cotton, 2012; Kuznekoff & Titsworth, 2013; Lepp, Barkley, & Karpinski, 2014; McCoy, 2013; Ophir et al., 2009; Rosen, Carrier, & Cheever, 2013; Tindell & Bohlander, 2012). In a discussion especially, this behavior is also extremely discourteous to both you and other students.

Therefore, consider banning the use of cell phones and laptops during discussion, unless you explicitly instruct your students to use them for some learning task, and enforce this ban with some kind of penalty for violations. To help ensure students' cooperation, you might want to give them a short break around the middle of the class period to check their cell phones (Cardon, 2014). When you do ask students to use cell phones or laptops in class to perform a specific task, such as research the answer to a question, allocate minimal time to keep students focused and have them work in small groups, three or four students to one device, because they probably won't be able to agree on a renegade site (Nilson & Weaver, 2005). Of course, you may ask individual students to take notes on their laptop to record the responses of their small group or the whole class, in which case they will be accountable to peers as well as you.

Challenge 7: Personal Attacks and Related Incivilities

A student's incivility can target you or other students, and we will deal with incivility against you as the instructor in this section. When it occurs, it will probably catch you off guard, leaving you without a ready response. You will feel angry, hurt, or both, but you can't show these emotions, and you must respond in a measured, rational way. So, plan for the occasion in advance.

Begin by keeping in mind that students' disrespectful behavior may have little to do with you and more to do with themselves or their perceptions of you. They may be immature, want attention, or have problems with authority. They may be testing you, pushing the envelope to see how far they can go before you get angry. Perhaps they have perceived you as being condescending, hostile, or cold, even if you never intended to convey this impression. Maybe they view you as weak and insecure, whether you feel that way or not. Some students make assumptions about faculty members, including their knowledge, experience, and teaching expertise, based on characteristics such as race, age, and gender, and it is important to recognize that stereotypes may be explicitly or implicitly driving some of this challenging student behavior.

What kinds of challenges might you face? A student may accuse you of wrongdoing, such as making an exam item "tricky" or being politically biased, racist, sexist, or offensive to his or her religious beliefs. Do not feel obliged to address the accusation during class. Just say you did not mean to give such an impression and are willing to discuss the issue privately outside of class. Then move on to the course material or other business at hand to avoid wasting other students' time. Also, you may want to confer with your chair, dean, campus office that handles student misconduct, and/or groups that oversee accusations of bias, and develop a clear action plan for how to respond to future accusations, particularly if you conclude together that the student either had nefarious intentions or that the student's class conduct was inappropriate. These colleagues can also advise you on next steps for addressing inappropriate student conduct at your institution and how and when to communicate those steps clearly to the student.

If a student challenges your legitimacy or acts in a way that disrupts the class—as can happen when a student comes to class drunk, insists on facing off with you immediately, and seems to be getting out of hand—tell the offender to leave the classroom for that day. If the student refuses to leave, call campus security. Taking swift, decisive action will discourage any would-be offenders (Carroll, 2003). Once the student leaves or is removed, review the incident with the other students in class so they can serve as witnesses. After class, write down exactly what happened and hold a meeting with your department chair to share your written record. If the hostility takes place out of class, try to move the confrontation into a public area. This action will help ensure you have witnesses and may quiet down the student. If the hostile behavior occurs in a discussion forum post, you have a written record but keeping the post up may disrupt the class. Therefore, delete it and contact the offending student to explain why you did (it's inappropriate, mean-spirited, unconstructive, uncalled for, etc.). Follow up by stating that another such post will result in your blocking the offender's future posts, which will impact his or her final course grade.

In a milder form of incivility, some students may try to pry answers out of you, especially before an exam. They may see this as easier than finding or working out the answer for themselves, or they may lack confidence in their own efforts. Either way, students need to obtain the correct answer on their own. During class or an online discussion, you can invite other students to provide hints or leads to the answer but *not* the answer. If this situation occurs one-on-one with you, answer each question with another question that should help the student recall or reason through the answer.

Challenge 8: Sensitive Subjects and Trigger Warnings

In chapter 2, we examined the importance of a positive course climate to discussion, particularly when addressing sensitive subjects or engaging in difficult conversations. Ambrose, Bridges, DiPietro, Lovett, and Norman (2010) explain that course climate is shaped by a number of factors, including stereotypes, tone, faculty-student and student-student interactions, and the inclusiveness of course content; how these elements impact the course is through how people interact with each other. Therefore, creating a positive climate involves setting expectations or guidelines for interactions, which establish a foundation to guide behavior in the class and will give you tools to address difficult conversations or sensitive subjects that may arise later. Some scholars use terms such as *safe spaces*, *respectful spaces*, or *free spaces* to describe strived-for interactions and the resulting classroom climate, as well as how these spaces are created or reinforced (Gayle, Cortez, & Preiss, 2013; Hadi & Sepler, 2016).

So how do you go about creating guidelines for how these spaces work? First, consider whether you will develop guidelines for interaction yourself or collaboratively with the students. In some instances, it may be helpful to draft a set of ground rules yourself and bring them to the class, such as first-year courses, large classes, or courses that have involved difficult classroom dynamics in the past. You can then discuss the ground rules with the students and invite them to add items. You may also want to include these expectations on the syllabus, incorporate them into your grading criteria and rubrics, post them on the wall, provide frequent verbal reminders, and model them through your own behavior. You may even revisit them occasionally and invite students to add to or amend them if needed. Another option is to involve students in collaboratively developing ground rules or course contracts (Center for Research on Learning and Teaching, n.d.; Herman & Nilson, 2016; Kustra & Potter, 2008; Quaye, 2012). In this approach, both your and your students' perceptions of what ideal interactions look like shape the framing and content of these expectations. This latter option requires more time and effort, particularly in larger classes, but it is more democratic and usually leads to greater student buy-in and a deeper understanding of the guidelines. This can take careful facilitation, though, particularly in a class in which students may never have created guidelines collaboratively before.

Once you have a process in mind, you can think about what content you might want to include. Realize that there aren't clear rules here: Faculty don't always agree on what the ideal is, nor may you and your students. Some examples of ground rules include the following:

- Treat others with respect.
- Don't ask others to speak for a larger group.
- Practice active listening; summarize another's perspective before adding your own.
- Maintain confidentiality in what is shared in the classroom.
- Recognize that intent and impact are different. You may have had a positive intent that has a negative impact on another person.
- Balance talking and listening. If you notice that you have been speaking more than others, allow space for others to join in the conversation.
- Don't interrupt someone who is speaking or engage in other conversation.
- Don't stereotype, label, blame, or judge.
- Challenge or criticize the idea, not the person. Don't "put down" people.
- If you have been impacted negatively by someone's words and would like this to be addressed, speak up (sometimes by saying "ouch").
- Speak only for yourself and your own experiences. Use "I" messages.
- Support your statements with evidence, data, and the readings.
- Respect others' rights to have opinions and beliefs that are different from your own.
- Be conscious of your body language and facial expressions and the nonverbal messages that they might convey.

Your colleagues may offer additional ideas. Also, realize that there is debate around what to include in these guidelines, leading to the different terms around *spaces* as described previously and questions like the following:

- To what degree can we promise or enforce confidentiality in a discussion?
- Can *safety* be interpreted as respectful dialogue, free from harassment or personal attacks? How can this be reinforced?
- Does *safety* mean comfort, and could it be inappropriate or detrimental to learning to try to shield students from negative emotions, sensitive topics, or opinions they don't endorse?
- How do these ideas mesh with legal or policy issues, such as disability accommodations or freedom of speech?

Regardless of how you might answer the preceding questions, what content you include in your guidelines, how you create them, or how you articulate them in your course, creating guidelines for how people interact in the class helps produce a positive course climate, which leads to effective discussion, and you can refer to these expectations when difficult discussions or sensitive topics arise.

Trigger warnings also enter into these debates around appropriate expectations for classroom interactions, especially discussion. Faculty may issue a written or verbal trigger warning before a class session; an activity; or some material that may contain potentially offensive or disturbing content to some students, particularly those who had a previous traumatic experience related to the subject. Some argue that trigger warnings improve course climate by excusing students who might suffer negative emotional repercussions by being retriggered or who have religious, moral, or personal objections to the content (Block, 2016; Lockhart, 2016). Others argue that excusing students from particular content negatively impacts their learning, poorly prepares them for handling uncomfortable topics later in life, and can even undermine their mental health (Jaschik, 2016; Lukianoff & Haidt, 2015; Vatz, 2016).

Clearly, you have a lot to think about when deciding how to frame expectations for interaction in a course, and discussion and research on these topics will continue to evolve. Considering these issues in the context of your discipline and course will help you shape the positive course climate that creates a supportive, safe environment for discussion.

Challenge 9: Microaggressions

When faculty members on our campuses ask about facilitating difficult conversations, their concerns often revolve around how to respond when a student makes a comment that a classmate may perceive as offensive or biased. These comments may involve incorrect information, implicit bias, poor understanding of a concept, tokenizing (asking a student to speak as a representative of a larger group), microaggressions, overt personal attacks, generalizations about larger groups, or unpleasant facts. Often these comments pertain to identity, particularly of marginalized groups, including race, class, gender, sexual orientation, national origin, religion, or age.

As with trigger warnings, the idea of microaggressions has set off debates, particularly about the types of comments or degrees of severity that warrant an instructor response or intervention. *Microaggressions*, defined as usually unintentional comments anchored in stereotypes of a particular group, have a cumulative negative effect on students over time (Sue, 2010), including on their learning. Many campuses have instituted bias response teams and protocols (Fernandes, 2016) in response to the increased emphasis on microaggressions, bias, and their negative impact on course climate and learning. These teams have based their actions on the impact on the person reporting the microaggression rather than on the intention of the person making the comment. However, some argue that microaggressions don't have a strong enough basis in research (Bartlett, 2017) and that "the increased focus on microaggressions [leads to] . . . a constant state of outrage, even toward well-meaning speakers trying to engage in genuine discussion," further leading to overreacting and seeking "punishment for anyone whose words make anyone feel uncomfortable" on some college campuses (Lukianoff & Haidt, 2015).

Your response to problematic student comments will be informed by your institution's culture and policies, your discipline, and your course content, and these few general guidelines may help. Do address the comment when it happens. Acknowledge it, but realize that rarely is a student's intent harmful, so avoid an accusatory approach. For example, if a student uses a term that others might find offensive, explain that a different term is preferred, and then move on. If a student makes a negative comment toward a classmate, such as name-calling, you can refer to the course ground rules or ask students to refrain from personal attacks. If appropriate for the course and discussion, you can also refer to the content to turn the problematic comment into a learning opportunity and to get the conversation back on track (Ambrose et al., 2010). Do respond calmly and rationally rather than emotionally (Warren, 2005), encourage students to do the same, and model inclusive language and behavior (Ambrose et al., 2010; Herman & Nilson, 2016). If emotions are running high, acknowledge them and calm the situation before proceeding, such as by asking the students to write for a few moments. If you think the comments were deliberate or particularly problematic, continue the conversation outside of class.

Challenge 10: Students With Autism Spectrum Disorder

College-level faculty members are beginning to see an increasing number of students with autism spectrum disorder (ASD) in their classrooms. Autism is an emotional and social disability that inhibits an individual from accurately reading or empathizing with the emotions of others or using the executive mental functions to regulate and moderate his or her behavior or emotional responses. These inabilities generate a host of serious challenges for the person, including loneliness, anxiety, depression, bullying, academic failure, housing/roommate problems, marginalization, a lack of situational understanding, inflexibility in routines and thinking patterns, a compulsion to be right, a low tolerance of ambiguity, an inability to grasp nuance, poor stress management, poor time management, poor inhibitory control, poor writing, disorganization, and an inability to generalize and process conceptually and globally (Corbett, Constantine, Hendren, Rocke, & Ozonoff, 2009; Gelbar, Smith, & Reichow, 2014; Gobbo & Shmulsky 2014; Hewitt, 2010; Mazefsky & White, 2014; S.W. White et al., 2016). It may be difficult to imagine what the world of a student with ASD is like.

Due to some of these challenges, these students often miss their instructors' and their classmates' nonverbal social cues. They may unknowingly violate the norms of discussion—for example, making comments on a prior subject, ignoring the instructor's directions, not making eye contact, disrupting class with inappropriate words or sounds, reacting angrily to students expressing a point of view different from theirs, interrupting speakers, dominating the discussion, or never contributing at all (Gobbo & Shmulsky, 2014).

Helping students with ASD better adjust to college has proven problematic. An intensive weeklong "camp" for entering students with high-functioning autism proved somewhat effective (Retherford & Schreiber, 2015), but a term-long course on social problem-solving did not (Pugliese & White, 2014). As an individual instructor, you can help somewhat by doing the following (Gobbo & Shmulsky, 2014):

- Be explicit in explaining your class format and expectations.
- Preview upcoming changes in your class.
- Be precise in asking discussion questions.
- Describe the type of desired response to questions.
- Give students with ASD a list of your discussion prompts in advance and ask them to prepare their responses before class.
- Meet individually with students with ASD to have them rehearse their answer to a discussion question that you will ask them during the next class.

Challenge 11: Asynchronous Online Discussions

The plethora of research on asynchronous online discussion, which is when students post to a discussion board at different times, documents many strategies for deriving its potential benefits. Such a discussion can build students' critical thinking, argument, and self-reflection skills (Al-Shalchi, 2009; M.D. Miller, 2014); promote engagement among introverted students (Howard, 2015); encourage the thoughtful integration of content; build community (Ruan & Griffith, 2011); and avoid the problems related to the traditional classroom, such as time limitations, dominating students, and large class sizes. It also effectively supports group collaboration, the implementation of problem-based learning, and case study approaches (Howard, 2015).

Nevertheless, asynchronous online discussion frequently incurs complaints about generating superficial or disconnected responses, feeling like an unengaging "chore" or busywork, and encouraging hostile or unproductive comments. No research has yet compared the quality and depth of asynchronous discussion comments in online versus in-person courses (Howard, 2015).

Most strategies for designing in-person discussion transfer smoothly to designing online discussion, such as closely connecting the discussion with learning objectives, providing clear and specific instructions, structuring tasks, assessing students' contributions against well-defined criteria, and setting ground rules for interaction. However, some strategies promote engagement specifically in asynchronous discussion, and we mention some here.

For instance, you can require students to post midweek and respond to each other's posts, but you must carefully word the questions you want them to answer (Palloff & Pratt, 2003), explicitly ask students to integrate the readings into their responses, and have clear criteria for assessing the contributions (Howard, 2015). Also see "Assessing Individual Students' Contributions" in chapter 5 for ways to involve students in their own self-assessment. You can also assign rotating "starter" and "wrapper" roles each week (M.D. Miller, 2014), ask students to generate prompts or test questions (M.D. Miller, 2014; Skibba, Moore, & Herman, 2013), and post strategically with a "light touch" (M.D. Miller, 2014, p. 147) to get students back on track. Three cases in this book, those of Marquart and Drury, Voegele, and Wilson (chapters 7, 12, and 13, respectively), provide detailed descriptions of their strategies for online discussion. We also recommend Howard (2015) for additional ideas on overcoming large classes, improving the quality of posts, building community, facilitating exchanges, and grading student contributions.

Challenge 12: Synchronous Online Discussions

In synchronous online discussion, discussion takes place in "real time" on an online platform, often the course management system. Synchronous discussions can either be text based, such as an online chat function, or rely on webcams to enable participants to both see and hear each other. These discussions are typically scheduled before the start of the course so that students can enroll knowing about this time commitment. Because institutions usually offer online courses with both time and geographic flexibility in mind, synchronous discussion tends to be less common than asynchronous (Howard, 2015).

Synchronous discussions incorporate many of the benefits of in-person discussion, including real-time interaction and small-group activities. However, some strategies mentioned in this chapter, such as those based on movement, do not transfer to online contexts, and connectivity problems, distractions from students' surroundings, and discomfort or unfamiliarity with the technology can pose challenges.

Still, you can leverage some of the strengths of synchronous online discussion to improve student learning. For example, online platforms typically incorporate participation tools that aren't available during in-person discussion, such as the ability to exchange and collaborate on documents during discussion, share views of each other's desktops, access and share online resources more readily, and simultaneously communicate orally or in writing.

Conclusion

The research-based strategies we have offered for preventing and responding to common pitfalls should help you successfully avert or stop the disruptions, inequities, and silences that can plague discussions. You can choose the strategies that you feel most comfortable using and experiment with different ones to find the most effective for your teaching environment and student population.

Engaging your students is only part of the task, however. Another part is ensuring that your students learn what you intend them to learn through the discussion, and the next chapter will help you achieve this objective.

4

CONNECTING DISCUSSION
WITH LEARNING

Jennifer H. Herman and Linda B. Nilson

An effective discussion creates a structure in which students are able to meet specific course learning objectives. However, many discussions are disconnected from the objectives, and students don't learn what the faculty member wanted them to learn. The following three scenarios illustrate how this disconnect can manifest in different disciplines.

Scenario 1: Discussion Is Superficial or Off Topic

In preparation for class, Professor Collins arranges 15 chairs in a circle for today's discussion on *Jane Eyre* (Bronte, 1847). Her British Literature II course is small and dominated by non–English majors who take the course to fulfill a humanities distribution requirement. Although her students complete the reading and seem to enjoy it, Professor Collins struggles to help them "get deeper" in class discussion, and today is no exception.

She begins the discussion by soliciting an overview of the book's plot and then asks the students, "Class conflict is clearly a central theme in this novel. What are some examples of how Jane perceives or struggles with class? Is she a conformist or a rebel? Do you think Brontë is critical of the class system, or is her perspective more analytical, more of a context for the characters' struggles?" The class is silent for a few moments and then students carefully share superficial comments:

"Well, her options are just so limited because of her class. I feel bad for her."

"She's always so careful since Mr. Rochester is high class and she isn't, and he's also her boss. It's not like dating your boss is a good idea today either; that hasn't changed a whole lot."

"She was also plain because she didn't have the money to buy fancy clothes or jewelry, so it affected her that way, too. It's easier to date if you have the funds."

Professor Collins sighs to herself again as the students veer off topic into discussing dating. It seems they don't even remember her original question and are more interested in socializing.

Scenario 2: Siloed Comments Dominate Discussion

Before class in his 200-level Global Health course, Professor Brussey assigned the article "Systems Thinking and Action for Nutrition" (SPRING, 2015) to give an overview of how various interconnected systems, such as policies, communications, infrastructure, and the sociocultural environment, shape nutrition. He asks the students to discuss in groups of three the meaning of *systems thinking* and to report out a summary of the idea along with their thoughts on which factor might have the biggest impact on an individual. He hopes that through debate the students will realize that there isn't one primary factor and that the different systems are, in fact, interconnected.

The students form triads, and Professor Brussey circulates while they discuss. He notices that students dive right in and are quickly engaged in arguing for their particular factor. He is pleased that they are using examples to support their argument—both from the reading and from real life—and really seem to understand how systems impact individuals. However, he soon notices that the students aren't recording or building on each other's ideas. They are impatiently waiting for whoever is speaking to finish and just jump into sharing their own idea without even acknowledging what was said before.

When he asks the groups to share, they begin by stating the definition of *systems thinking* from the article. Then, the reporter states that "many ideas were discussed," shares his or her own idea, and then notes that they did not come to consensus. With 10 groups, the reporting out is long and tedious, and much of the content is repetitive. Students are clearly not listening, and Professor Brussey is frustrated that they never got the larger point.

Scenario 3: Discussion Is Based on Opinion, Biased, or Not Supported by Data

In her Introduction to Gender Studies course, Professor Weckle has just finished an overview of the adoption of *they* as a singular, gender-neutral pronoun by the *Associated Press Stylebook* in March 2017 and the American Dialect Society's declaration of the singular *they* as the Word of the Year in

2016. Professor Weckle then places the students in groups of six and asks them to discuss the potential impact of this formal legitimizing of the singular *they* on gender-nonconforming people and the acceptance of gender-neutral language. Once in their groups, the students begin sharing personal experiences with gender-neutral language, naming people they know who use the singular *they* and describing their interactions with those individuals. The students also share their own pronoun preferences and talk about other gender-neutral pronouns that they've heard. Some of them speculate how the legitimization of *they* might emotionally impact people who use that pronoun. Others voice the opinion that this is just a trend and other ways of referring to people will emerge, while still others argue that the word "just isn't grammatically correct," despite what the Associated Press or the American Dialect Society says. Professor Weckle is frustrated: She feels that the students' comments are based on their opinions or personal experiences and that they are not using any evidence to back up their ideas. She observes that some of the unsupported comments are not only biased but actually contradictory to her message about the current evolution of language toward the acceptance of gender-neutral terminology.

In each of these scenarios, the learning objective wasn't clear, and different challenges emerged that created a disconnect between the instructor's goal for the discussion and the actual learning that took place. In Scenario 1, the contributions were superficial and off topic; the students didn't engage in the complex analysis of class that Professor Collins was hoping for. In Scenario 2, the quest to have the right answer led to students not listening to each other and just waiting for their turn to speak. The discussion didn't build off each contributor's ideas to lead to a deeper understanding, as Professor Brussey anticipated. Finally, in Scenario 3, Professor Weckle's students shared opinions and ideas that were not supported by evidence, and in some ways the discussion contradicted what she was trying to teach.

Each of these scenarios demonstrates how important it is to design a discussion so that students are actually learning the content of the course. This chapter will provide a framework for designing discussions within the larger course context. At the end of the chapter, we will revisit these three scenarios and suggest alternative methods of designing each discussion so that students reach the intended objective.

Connecting Discussion and Learning

As the three scenarios illustrate, discussion as a pedagogical tool can fail to lead students to achieve the planned learning objectives for the course. How do you avoid this failure? Unfortunately, creating an effective discussion to meet learning objectives doesn't follow an easy recipe in a "tips and tricks" guide, a process described in a published case study, or a method used in a colleague's classroom. Sometimes attempting to reproduce another's success in your own course works, but often it doesn't. The best designed and most successful discussions cannot be cut and pasted from another context but rather are built into the course as part of a larger course design process. This larger design must come first to delineate the most useful cases and examples and to furnish clear, course-specific guidelines for selecting and adapting others' successes to your own context.

The next section of this chapter explains how to incorporate discussion into the larger course design, using the proven backward design model (Fink, 2013; Wiggins & McTighe, 1998). We will explain how learning objectives, assessments, and other teaching methodologies should drive decisions about when and why discussion belongs in your course. This initial step emphasizes understanding and articulating the *function* of the discussion within the larger course design. Then you can plan the *structure* of the discussion within a particular class session or learning unit using the successful models and approaches of others.

The alignment between course design and discussion design determines the effectiveness of discussion in helping students learn. As the three scenarios show, discussion is likely to fail pedagogically if disconnected from the broader course design. So please read and apply the framework and process described in this chapter.

Discussion as Part of Course Design

Selecting and incorporating discussion as a teaching methodology is one of the last steps of a broader course design process that centers around learning objectives. Wiggins and McTighe (1998) developed the process of *backward design* originally for the K–12 system. Five years later, Fink (2003, 2013) reframed the approach for higher education as *integrated course design* in *Creating Significant Learning Experiences: An Integrated Approach to Designing College Courses*. Biggs and Tang (2011) also wrote a text focused on *constructive alignment* for higher education course design based on a similar process. As the backward design process has proven popular and successful in fostering student learning in higher education (Fink, 2003), we use it to explain how to integrate discussion as an effective teaching methodology.

Step 1: Aligning Discussion With Learning Objectives

Backward design begins with identifying the student learning objectives (or outcomes) for your course. In other words, what do you want your students to be able to do by the end of your course or some shorter unit? We often think in terms of the content that they should master, but what should they be able to *do* with that content? What cognitive skills should they develop? What social or ethical skills? What affective or values-based goals should they attain? Clearly articulating these learning objectives is a necessary first step to clarify the purpose that discussion will serve in your course.

Because all courses have cognitive skills, let's first home in on these. Although discussion can help students meet lower level learning objectives, such as remembering and understanding (Anderson & Krathwohl, 2001; Bloom, 1956), chapter 1 in this book lists many more complex learning benefits of discussion—in particular, higher level thinking (applying, analyzing, evaluating, and creating), problem-solving, inquiry, questioning, communication, and retention of the material. In terms of Bloom's taxonomy, the cognitive level of the key verb in the objective will impact what tasks or questions you give to the students. Depending upon this level, you might ask students to summarize an argument, explain a key concept, give a novel example, analyze how a system works, evaluate data to support an argument, listen actively, or debate a controversial issue using evidence during a discussion. All of these cognitive operations should help students deepen their understanding of a complex concept or multifaceted issue.

If one or more of your learning objectives is social, such as building students' skills to work effectively on a team, the questions or content involved in the discussion matter less than the appropriate discussion processes—for example, how you set up the teams and help them learn to manage themselves. If one of your objectives is ethical, another purpose discussion serves well (see chapter 1), you will want students to analyze the moral ramifications of various courses of action.

Discussion also helps foster interest in the material and motivation to learn it; citizenship; and open-mindedness to new beliefs, values, ideas, and behaviors—all of which represent affective objectives (see chapter 1). Suskie (2009) includes appreciation, integrity, valuing learning, and self-awareness in these goals. In discussion, you can ask students to examine new ideas and information and to reflect on how these deepen their understanding of a complex issue or challenge or change their previously held assumptions. Such a discussion benefits from opportunities for individual feedback in advance; anonymous contributions; think-pair-share opportunities; small-group exchanges; rules for respectful dialogue; and careful facilitation to ensure contributions are heard, acknowledged, and considered.

Regardless of the types of learning objective, you can strengthen a discussion by designing both its structure and its content to explicitly meet the objective(s). Explaining the discussion's goals and design to the students can also help them understand how it fits into the bigger picture of what they are

learning in your course and other educational experiences and lead to endur-
ing learning (Maki, 2010).

Step 2: Using Discussion to Support Assessment

The second step in the backward design process—developing graded assignments or nongraded activities to determine how well the students have met
the learning objectives—also impacts discussion design. The assessments
answer the question, "How do you know that they know?," which Jane Vella
(2002) raised in *Learning to Listen, Learning to Teach.* Discussion can serve
to help students prepare for an assessment, assess the learning itself, or both.
Most commonly, discussion serves the former purpose. In this case, you
should explain the learning objective to the students; give an overview of
the paper, quiz, or other assessment method; and clarify how discussion will
help prepare them to do well on that assessment. Seeing this connection will
motivate students to fully engage in the discussion.

As an assessment method, discussion can provide both you and your
students with either formative feedback (a measure of students' progress)
or summative feedback (an end-of-learning assessment). As Vella (2002)
advises, assessments supply the strongest data when they are *authentic* (from
real life), *observable* (students say or produce something), and *measurable*
(you can judge the quality) indicators of the degree to which each student
has achieved an objective. If you intend to summatively assess (grade) the
discussion as a whole or the contributions of its participants, see chapter 5
for various strategies.

Step 3: Improving Discussion by Setting Performance Expectations

After the learning objectives and assessments are in place, the third step in the
course design process is to articulate the level of performance that you want
the students to achieve. What does success look like? Many faculty members develop a rubric to help them articulate their expectations in writing.
Creating a rubric requires you to clearly identify the knowledge, skills, and
affective context that students will need for the assessment. You begin by listing the criteria by which you will judge the quality of the students' work and
then describe "acceptable" and "excellent" work for each criterion (Stevens &
Levi, 2012). All students should perform acceptable work to meet the learning objectives and pass the course, although excellent work remains the ideal.

If you are using discussion as a pedagogical tool to help prepare students
for an assessment, you should integrate the criteria and their acceptable level
into your discussion design. For example, let's say that one of your objectives
is for students to analyze the charter school funding debate, and you will

assess this through an argument paper. Your rubric includes the criterion that students use reputable sources of evidence to support their argument. Therefore, for the preparatory discussion, have students bring three pieces of evidence with them and evaluate each source in small groups on how scholarly, reputable, free of bias, and supportive of their argument it is. If students understand that the discussion will help them write a better paper, they will have more reason to engage in and focus on the discussion.

If discussion figures into your course grades, then developing and sharing with students a clear rubric with your criteria and expectations can motivate better preparation and stronger engagement in the discussion. Your criteria can include, for example, using readings or outside sources to support a claim, building explicitly off a classmate's ideas, or asking questions that help deepen the complexity of the conversation. No doubt, developing a rubric will result in a higher quality discussion with a stronger connection to learning (see chapter 5).

Step 4: Using Discussion as a Teaching Methodology

In this fourth and final step of the backward design process, you select teaching methodologies that help prepare students for each of the assessments. How do you know what to select and when to include discussion? In *Creating Significant Learning Experiences*, Fink (2013) introduces learning activities for active, holistic learning, which include gathering new information and ideas, gaining experience by observing and doing, and reflecting in dialogue with oneself or others. Discussion can serve any of these purposes: The jigsaw method (see chapter 2) helps students acquire and understand new information, debates and task-based discussions add experience, and thought-focused discussion encourages reflective dialogue.

In her course design workshops, Herman presents a framework of content-experience-reflection (C-E-R). She derived it from Fink's categorization of learning activities to foster thinking about the role of discussion in a course. In the C-E-R framework, each cohesive learning experience must contain three components: the introduction of new content, direct experience engaging actively with the content, and reflection that enables the learner to analyze the content through the lens of the active learning experience. The C-E-R framework also draws upon Kolb's (1984) experiential learning cycle, particularly the idea that learners learn best from experience through reflection.

When designing a class using the C-E-R framework, first identify the breadth of each learning experience, which is often one class and the related homework you assign before or after the class. (You can also stipulate that the learning experience encompasses several class sessions.) Then consider how you can apply a C-E-R structure across multiple learning units to add coherence and predictability to your course.

To illustrate, you typically deliver the first part of the framework, content, through readings, videos, websites, or lectures, either inside or outside class. But discussion can also deliver content, such as when each student shares an article, new knowledge, or personal experience with the group. More broadly, you might want to decide how and when students typically get content and build that into your framework. For example, you can regularly have students view a recorded lecture and read a selection before class and then allow class time for discussion and other activities. You can also have a routine of sharing content through lecture and then having students briefly discuss the content for clarity and comprehension—an excellent strategy to reduce cognitive load and increase understanding in large, content-heavy lecture courses. Regardless, having a pattern of content delivery and discussion throughout the course will help create greater coherence and predictability.

Experience, the second part of the C-E-R framework, encompasses a wide range of active learning teaching methods: simulations, role-playing, case studies, problem-based learning, debate, lab work, interviewing, project-based learning, problem-solving, writing to learn, and many others. Sometimes these activities use discussion as the mechanism for the experience, such as debate, interviews, or group work. Experience activities often take place during class but also make viable out-of-class assignments, such as service-learning, skill practice, and group projects.

The third and final piece of the C-E-R framework, reflection, allows students to connect content and experience in a meaningful way. It can take place inside or outside class as an individual or a group activity. With its focus on meaning-making (Fink, 2013), it can assume many forms, such as writing a reflection paper on a service-learning project, writing up lab results, or answering essay questions on an exam, all of which represent individual reflections. Discussion is the most common form of group reflection, whether done in a large class or small groups, and can also take various forms: debriefing an experience, analyzing it against a best practice example or a rubric, sharing reactions to an experience, connecting it with prior experience, interpreting it using content, or getting or giving feedback to others.

In the backward design model, selecting discussion as a teaching method takes place during this final step. By this time, you know what learning objective(s) discussion helps support; how discussion prepares students to perform well on the assessments; which specific content, skills, attitudes, or values the students are gaining from the discussion and for which assessments; and whether you intend the discussion to deliver new content, create an active learning experience, or facilitate reflection to connect new content with a learning experience.

Backward Design of the Learning Unit and Discussion

Once you design your course as a whole, you can start developing the learning units and the discussion activities using the same backward design process. For an individual learning unit, you first articulate clear learning objectives. Do you hope students will develop a deeper understanding of a concept in the reading? That they will be able to analyze a role play experience based on theories from the literature? Compare and interpret results from two different data analysis techniques? Focus on the *verb* in the learning objective—what you want the students to *do*.

If you decide discussion can help students meet your learning objectives, then decide what role discussion will play in relation to the course's assessments. Does the discussion prepare students for a future assignment, or will the discussion itself serve as the assessment of learning? If discussion is the form of assessment, are you using this to gauge students' progress, or are you grading them on their results? Have you articulated, on a rubric or elsewhere, what an acceptable level of performance looks like either for the discussion or for the future assessment for which the discussion is preparing students? Have you communicated those expectations to the students? How will the criteria in your rubric inform how you construct your discussion?

Next, consider the C-E-R framework for this unit. What role should discussion play—content, experience, or reflection? Should certain content or experience precede or follow the discussion? Do students need to gain any knowledge or develop any skills through the discussion that are directly tied to the "acceptable" or "excellent" results that you are seeking on a related assignment?

Finally, use the strategies and insights from the 12 principles to design your individual discussion session. We also recommend drawing ideas from the case studies in this book (chapters 6–13) to help you structure your discussion. Let's now turn back to the three examples that opened this chapter and consider how applying backward design to the learning unit and discussion design can help improve outcomes for student learning.

Reconnecting Discussion and Learning: Redesigning the Three Scenarios

For each of the three scenarios at the beginning of this chapter, we will walk through a redesign to improve the connection between discussion and the content, applying principles described in this chapter.

In the first scenario, Professor Collins struggles with her students' superficial discussion of class difference in *Jane Eyre* before they veer off topic altogether. Although they seem interested in the content (they did the reading!), she has many non–English majors who may not understand how she intends the discussion to further the course's learning goals. Professor Collins needs to formulate clear learning goals for the discussion and then share them with students.

Although willing to speak up, her students only mention points related to class issues from the novel. This is recall and understanding, the step *before* deeper analytic work. Following the backward design process, Professor Collins can tie a future paper to the learning objectives, describe her performance expectations for the paper to the students, and explain how the discussion can help them prepare for this assignment. Then she can suggest how they should get ready for the discussion in advance—perhaps by listing manifestations of class in the novel or prewriting answers to the discussion questions—so they can explore the novel on a deeper level in class.

In Professor Brussey's Global Health course, students fail to build on each other's ideas and miss the larger point, leading to a tedious reporting process. To his credit, Professor Brussey knows what he wants students to learn to do through the discussion: to derive and interconnect the system factors impacting individuals. However, for the discussion, he directs students simply to summarize the meaning of systems thinking and decide which factor has the biggest impact. He would like debate, but he asks students to come to consensus.

The students use evidence to support their ideas and initially share with enthusiasm, but the discussions quickly dissolve into siloed comments as the students realize that the professor has asked for consensus around the one right answer. Their eagerness to be right and win the competition kicks in, so they stop listening to each other. Because they don't move beyond sharing possibilities and lack the criteria to judge what the best answer may be, they just report out ideas without much analysis.

Professor Brussey could avoid this problem by framing the discussion more carefully to meet his learning objective. For example, he could use the C-E-R approach and connect discussion more explicitly with the content (the assigned article). He could prepare his students by having them outline the main points before class and select the most cogent points in their groups. He also could use a case study, such as a scenario about a person in a specific context suffering from malnutrition, and ask the students to analyze how systems might impact that person's situation. Student groups could share their results in ways other than reporting out—for example, creating a concept map, which would also help them connect their ideas.

In the third scenario, Professor Weckle is dismayed that her students are exchanging personal experiences and drawing from unsupported opinions and biased perspectives rather than using evidence to back up their ideas. She worries that some of their comments may actually contradict what she is try-ing to teach. Although she regards the discussion as unsuccessful, it is actually following her request that the students talk about the potential impact of the formal legitimizing of the singular *they* on gender-nonconforming people and the acceptance of gender-neutral language. The students are merely shar-ing examples of the impact on people whom they know and explaining their own degrees of acceptance of gender-neutral language.

Professor Weckle hoped that the conversation would draw on evidence and theory to explore the larger, more systemic impact of the language change. This is another example in which the instructor should have announced her intended learning objective and perhaps modeled a few suitable comments. She also could have used the C-E-R framework. If students are reflecting on content during this discussion, where are they drawing the content from? Professor Weckle provides a helpful overview of how language is changing, but unless the students have read sources that speak to the broader implica-tions of this change, they won't have much content to draw from except personal experience. In the future, she can connect the discussion more explicitly with scholarly content and model how to use evidence to avoid personal opinion and address the issue at a national, rather than personal, level. She can also apply backward design to link the discussion to an upcom-ing assignment that asks students to use evidence in a similar way and explain how this discussion will give them practice in evidence-based thinking.

All three of these scenarios show that discussion can result in learning if properly planned and guided. Like every other teaching method, discussion requires one or more learning objectives to serve an instructional purpose. We wouldn't introduce a problem-based learning experience, a role-play, a simulation, or a group assignment into a course without a learning objec-tive in mind, nor would we have students write a paper, design an energy-efficient building, or construct a rocket prototype for no specific learning purpose. A discussion deserves the same care and attention.

5

GAUGING THE
EFFECTIVENESS OF
A DISCUSSION

Jennifer H. Herman and Linda B. Nilson

The idea of assessing a discussion may seem novel; the topic rarely appears in the literature. However, we really need to know how well a discussion has engaged our class, and we need data that are more reliable than just the amount of participation we can vaguely recall. We also need to know how effectively a discussion has met our learning objectives for the session. If we don't find out these things, how will we be able to improve our discussions or know whether they are effective in the first place?

In this chapter we examine three areas of effectiveness that need assessment: how engaged the class overall is in a discussion, how well the discussion advances the learning objectives or content, and the quality and quantity of individual student contributions.

Assessing Class Engagement and Participation in a Discussion

With little published guidance on assessing a discussion as a whole, we have to draw most of our ideas from those strategies used in the cases in chapters 6 through 13 and our own personal experience. So how did the faculty in our cases assess their classes' engagement and participation in discussions? How did they gauge the breadth of this engagement and participation, not individual student contributions? The variety of approaches may be surprising. Of course, the following suggestions represent just a sample of the possible strategies imaginable.

- Monitor student participation grades in an online or face-to-face class (Marquart & Drury, chapter 7). (The section later in this chapter "Assessing Individual Students' Contributions" addresses ways to evaluate individual participation.) This method assumes that you use the same measure of individual participation throughout a class and in each course offering.
- Monitor whether student enrollment increases in later offerings of a classroom or online course (Marquart & Drury, chapter 7). However, remember that course enrollments may change due to other factors.
- Have students prepare for the discussion by writing responses to specific questions (in this case, in online journals on which the instructor may comment) to be shared and analyzed during the discussion to identify themes, which then become prompts for written reflections. This structured technique is called *collaborative autoethnography* (CAE) (Shapiro, chapter 8). With the responses in front of them, even reticent students would find it relatively easy to participate.
- Keep count of the number of different students who make a contribution during a face-to-face class or online discussion and then calculate the proportion of participating students (Shewmaker, chapter 9). When used in a face-to-face class, this method assumes that you are calling on volunteers. When many different students participate, overall class engagement is high.
- Keep count of the number of classroom or online discussions during which more than two or three students dominate (Shewmaker, chapter 9). Again, this method in a face-to-face class assumes that you are calling on volunteers. A discussion dominated by only two or three students demonstrates little overall class engagement.
- Monitor the apparent level of excitement and passion during a discussion, which the amount of student movement, debate, and noise level may indicate (Townsend, chapter 11). This indicator is quite subjective but can still be valid.
- Ask students to evaluate the degree of community among them, whether in an online or face-to-face class (Voegele, chapter 12). Of course, other factors can influence a perceived sense of community, such as how well students in the class know each other from other contexts.
- Monitor the lengths of posts during an online discussion; longer posts indicate higher engagement (Wilson, chapter 13). The type of discussion question will also affect the length of the posts.

- Have students write evaluations of the overall participation in the discussion at the end of the class or as homework (authors' experience; McGonigal, 2005). Although each student's evaluation may be subjective, the collective class opinion may come close to reality.
- Ask students to write evaluations of their own contribution to the discussion, followed by strategies to improve their contributions (authors' experience; McGonigal, 2005). You need to supply your students with criteria on which to evaluate and improve their contributions. For suggested criteria, see the section later in this chapter, "Assessing Individual Students' Contributions."

Assessing a Discussion's Effectiveness in Helping Students Meet Course Learning Objectives

A discussion can evoke a great deal of student participation but go off topic, skim over the material superficially, not meet the learning objectives, or otherwise fail to advance students' learning in the way it was intended. This learning may emphasize mastery of the course content or the development of specific skills, such as active listening, argument analysis, use of evidence to back up claims, use of the language of the discipline, or critical thinking. Therefore, assessing a discussion's effectiveness in helping students meet the course learning objectives is another important task. Unfortunately, the literature offers some but not much advice here.

Conderman (2017) asks a question at the beginning of class to gauge his students' level of knowledge or confidence on the topic of the day and the same or a related question at the end. For example, a discussion might start with this prompt (ours, not Conderman's):

> We've been reading about several species that went extinct through the ages and why they did. Why should we try to save species before they go extinct, or should we? Why shouldn't we just let nature take its course? Even if humans had something to do with the extinction, aren't we a part of nature?

After students have listened to and debated a range of positions, the discussion might close with these related questions: What is your stance on the issue of species preservation? Should we try to preserve species that are going extinct or not? Does it depend? If so, on what?

Conderman's pretest/posttest approach has scientific appeal, but remember that your assessment of a class period is an informal tool for you to improve your teaching and should be an organic part of the discussion.

McGonigal (2005) suggests a number of ways to assess student learning in a discussion. One is simply to have students complete a written assignment at the end of the class. If students have missed or misconstrued major points, you can revisit the topic later and give them a follow-up assignment. Another is to require students to post a response on an online discussion board to a question that formed the spine of the discussion. You can also ask students to evaluate the quality of the discussion, describe how it solved a problem, or reflect on how the discussion changed their understanding or thinking on the main topic. If the class addressed a controversy or disagreements emerged, ask students to summarize the conflict, assess how effectively the discussion handled it, and explain their own perspective on the issue. Students can respond to any of these questions in writing at the end of class, in a homework assignment, or on a follow-up online discussion board (McGonigal, 2005).

All of our cases in the next several chapters use various methods to assess the effectiveness of a discussion in helping students advance their mastery of the content. At the end of the following list, we add our own experience in assessing discussions.

- Have students informally write responses to prompts asking how their thinking and understanding changed or deepened due to the discussion (Festle, chapter 6). This method also provides students with a valuable metacognitive exercise.
- Have students post their list of takeaways from the discussion (Marquart & Drury, chapter 7). This activity also has metacognitive value.
- Ask students for anonymous feedback about the quality of the discussion (Marquart & Drury, chapter 7). Students may not know the characteristics of a high-quality discussion and will need a list or rubric from you. You can also lead a first-day discussion on what students have experienced as a high-quality discussion.
- Assign and assess individual papers in which students draw on their CAE journals to create their own model of leadership identity development (Shapiro, chapter 8). You can adapt this assessment technique to your course if you have your students keep a pre- or postdiscussion journal of their learning that they use in a paper or project that they develop individually.
- Keep track of the quality of the student comments in terms of how well they demonstrate deep, accurate understanding of the concepts as compared to the comments in previous offerings of the course. This increase in student learning seems to increase participation as well,

perhaps because students have higher confidence in their command of the material (Shewmaker, chapter 9). This method assumes you have at least an informal record of the comments in previous course offerings.

- Use classroom assessment techniques (e.g., one-minute paper and four-square, which poses four questions about the discussion experience) at the end of class. In addition, assess students' conceptual understanding and application skills on papers and exams (Strean, chapter 10). This assessment is not comparative, except to your own expectations.

- Assign a major research project and observe improvements in students' research skills, from total unfamiliarity to being able to locate and read journal articles (Townsend, chapter 11). This method examines students' growth as researchers.

- Survey students on how they benefited from the major assignment around which discussions took place (Townsend, chapter 11). This method homes in on students' self-assessment as researchers.

- Have students write critical reflections on what they gained from the face-to-face and online discussions, with an emphasis on their sense of class community, their ability to integrate the discussions on both platforms, and their perceived depth of the understanding of course concepts (Voegele, chapter 12). To ensure students have an accurate memory of the discussions, they must write these reflections shortly afterward.

- Keep track of the quality of posts compared to posts in previous offerings of the course (Wilson, chapter 13). You must have a record of the posts from one or more previous course offerings. This assessment strategy echoes Shewmaker's (chapter 9) discussed previously, although hers is in a face-to-face course and Wilson's is in an online course.

- Give a short-essay quiz at the end of class that assesses how well students have achieved the ultimate outcome(s) of the discussion (authors' experience). To help students pay attention, inform them in advance about these objectives and the quiz they will take later.

- Have students reflect how well the discussion met its goals (authors' experience). Of course, you must articulate these goals at the beginning of class.

Assessing Individual Students' Contributions

We already described many strategies for assessing the degree of *class* engagement and in the learning value of a discussion, but you may also want to evaluate the quality of the contributions of your individual students, especially if you are grading them on their participation. The literature offers three different approaches to this task, all of which work well across the disciplines. The first involves developing and using a *participation rubric* (Kustra & Potter, 2008); the second, having students keep, submit, and evaluate a *participation log* (Docan-Morgan, 2015); and the third, having students keep, submit, and grade a *participation portfolio* (Division of Information Technology, University of Maryland Baltimore County, n.d.). A rubric also pairs well with the other two approaches, but Kustra and Potter (2008) intend that *you* use it to grade participation, whereas the participation log and the participation portfolio have *students* use the respective tools to self-assess.

Kustra and Potter (2008) make a strong case for using a rubric to assess the discussion skills and contributions of individual students. They explain the many good purposes that a good rubric serves: focusing your attention on the objectives you want students to achieve in the discussion, and more broadly, the course; minimizing any grading biases; making your expectations explicit; helping students understand and meet your expectations; and increasing rigor in grading.

You must carefully consider the criteria you will use because you shouldn't burden students with more than six, and you have many options, including the following:

- quantity/frequency of contributions;
- listening skills;
- accuracy of content;
- demonstration of knowledge gained from assigned material;
- relevancy/responsiveness to the discussion issues;
- insight into discussion issues;
- demonstration of higher level thinking (e.g., analyzes critically, draws inferences, solves problems, makes comparisons and connections, draws conclusions, critically evaluates);
- evidence offered to support claims;
- sense of community fostered;
- professionalism;
- responsiveness to instructor feedback;
- responsiveness to student feedback; and
- quality of follow-up responses and feedback to other students.

In face-to-face discussions, you may also want to take delivery, such as audibility and eye contact, into account, whereas in online discussions, you may want to include the timeliness of posts, post length, student adherence to online protocols and netiquette, post clarity, mechanics, and even references. You can weight each criterion equally or differentially; just be sure you explain the different levels of quality (three to five) for each one.

For rubric models and examples, simply type "sample participation rubric" into a search engine. The Web contains dozens of rubrics that you can access for free (e.g., Augustine and Culture Seminar, 2008; Eberly Center for Teaching Excellence, n.d.; Maznevski, 1996; Oregon Health & Science University, n.d.; Stanny, 2010; University of Northern Arizona e-Learning Center, 2016; University of Wisconsin, Green Bay, n.d.; Vandervelde, 2016). Table 5.1 is an example rubric that adopts and modifies elements from many of the participation rubrics that are available online.

The *participation log* eases much of the burden of trying to track student participation accurately in the classroom and online (Docan-Morgan, 2015; Rogers, n.d.). To implement it, you distribute a form that asks students to report specifically what they contributed to a whole-class discussion or lecture or to a small-group discussion or activity and on what day, as well as how their contribution aided the progression or the interaction. In addition, you should request two self-assessments during the semester in which students identify their strengths and ways for them to improve both the quantity and quality of their participation. According to its developer, Docan-Morgan (2015), your syllabus should outline your participation expectations, such as at least one contribution weekly with connections to the assigned readings, or include a participation rubric. You must also inform students from the first day of the course that they will be recording and evaluating their contributions on a simple form that you provide. You should give your own written feedback on each student's participation on at least the first form they submit. By helping you view the discussions through your students' eyes, both self-assessments can help you improve your discussion questioning and management skills.

The *participation portfolio* also streamlines the grading process for online discussion (Division of Information Technology, University of Maryland Baltimore County, n.d.). At the beginning of the course, you furnish a participation rubric that specifies what constitutes quality contributions and replies. As with the participation log, you must also inform students that they will be recording and evaluating their contributions. Every two to four weeks, students submit in writing a number of examples—two, three, or four, your choice—of their best contributions or replies along with a collective grade, which you can then accept, raise, or lower. This technique not only saves you grading time but also frees you from tracking student participation. At Baltimore County's website, you will find detailed instructions and can watch a demonstration (University of Maryland, Baltimore, n.d.).

TABLE 5.1

Example of a Rubric to Assess Individual Students' Participation in Discussions

Criterion Level	Mature/ Exemplary	Satisfactory/ Good	Developing	Unacceptable
Preparation for discussion	Shows deep understanding of the readings and frequently refers to them for ideas, evidence, and perspectives	Usually shows good understanding of the readings and refers to them for ideas, evidence, and perspectives	Shows superficial understanding of the readings or infrequently refers to them	Shows little or no evidence of doing the readings on a regular basis
Quality of thought demonstrated in contributions	Analyzes, synthesizes, or evaluates course material on a regular basis and advances the discussion in new directions	Occasionally analyzes, synthesizes, or evaluates course material deeply enough to advance the discussion	Repeats information from course material, showing little thought about the ideas or perspectives	Makes superficial, disruptive, or irrelevant comments, or none at all
Frequency of participation	Makes multiple high-quality contributions every discussion without dominating it	Makes at least one high-quality contribution almost every discussion	Occasionally makes a worthwhile contribution	Rarely or never makes a worthwhile contribution
Sense of community encouraged	Consistently attentive and respectful when other students contribute; makes eye contact with them and does not interrupt, roll eyes, or show disdain*	Generally attentive and respectful when other students contribute; usually makes eye contact with them*	Occasionally attentive when other students contribute; makes little eye contact with them*	Inattentive to what other students contribute; fails to make eye contact or interrupts, rolls eyes, or shows disdain*

(Continues)

TABLE 5.1 (*Continued*)

Criterion Level	Mature/ Exemplary	Satisfactory/ Good	Developing	Unacceptable
Quality of feedback to other students	Makes multiple high-quality comments on the contributions of other students every or almost every discussion; builds on contributions, asks questions about them, or tactfully critiques them	Regularly makes comments on the contributions of other students, but the comments may vary in quality	Occasionally comments on the contributions of other students, and the comments vary in quality	Does not comment, at least not constructively, on the contributions of other students

*Applies only to face-to-face discussions.

Reducing Risk, Enhancing Value

The idea of assessing the discussions you build into your courses merits your attention because discussion can be a high-risk teaching method. When discussion fails to elicit your students' participation or advance their learning, it can negatively impact engagement in the rest of the course. With so many different ways of assessing a discussion's success in engaging students and furthering their learning, you can experiment with different options. Most of them will take very little time, and all of them will help you develop a better rapport with your students and make better use of class time.

6

LEARNING AND INTERPRETING HISTORY THROUGH DELIBERATIVE DIALOGUE

Mary Jo Festle

I face multiple challenges in teaching the face-to-face history survey course The United States Since 1865. One challenge is that many of the students, who are almost all nonhistory majors, mistakenly assume that history primarily involves memorizing an endless, boring, and indisputable string of names and dates. Many are surprised by the threshold concept that historians actually interpret the past and make arguments about how to judge and characterize events. Students need practice in making thoughtful interpretations using facts as evidence to bolster their arguments.

I am also challenged to introduce students to historically important concepts and skills that students will find useful after college. One such concept is that people experienced the past differently based on who they were. Because it is difficult to shift our lens to that of others, and because perspective taking is a foundational skill for developing intercultural competence (Deardorff, 2011), I want to give students practice making this shift.

My final challenge is facilitating sustained and thoughtful discussion in which almost all of the students participate. In smaller classes and those populated by more advanced students, I don't have a problem with this. To my dismay, however, my attempts at facilitating a whole-class discussion with a group larger than 25 students had fallen into a pattern more like a fact-based recitation dominated by a handful of ever-ready students than an in-depth discussion of ideas by an engaged majority. I know how to stimulate energetic debates, but I want to avoid the sort of polarized debates that students see in popular media, characterized by talking over one another, exaggeration of positions, and manipulation of evidence. These so-called debates result in much heat but little light. I want students to leave a discussion feeling that, thanks to their classmates, they've deepened their understanding of the issues, rather than feeling that they have won or lost a competition.

Deliberative dialogue is a method that helps me address all three challenges. While there are varying models for processes involving deliberation and dialogue, summarized in a framework by the National Coalition for Dialogue & Deliberation (2014), the method I tried is a structured format in which participants systematically and respectfully consider different perspectives of the various stakeholders. The term *dialogue* implies that participants learn through an interactive process with others, which is an exchange (not a monologue) in which they share and listen to one another's ideas, experiences, values, and viewpoints. *Deliberative* refers to both the (deliberate) pace of the process and the manner in which the process is carried out: intentionally, carefully, and respectfully. Deliberate dialogue aims to bring into the open the different values and reasoning of participants who weigh multiple positions and deliberately consider the pros and cons and implications of each position. Often communities (towns, organizations, universities) use this process for discussing contemporary problems or political controversies, hoping to find some common ground on which to base future actions. I wondered if it might be adapted to discussing problems in and differing interpretations about the past.

I decided to try deliberative dialogue after a workshop sponsored by North Carolina Campus Compact, which shares materials for how to conduct one (North Carolina Campus Compact, n.d.). The facilitators, Jill McMillan and John Llewellyn, shared their experiences at Wake Forest University, where they held a campus-wide dialogue and also sponsored a group of 30 Democracy Fellows who had participated in a 4-year program involving class, campus, and community-wide dialogues. A longitudinal investigation showed that experience with the dialogues helped the Democracy Fellows develop more agency in and dispositions toward democracy. They believed that the skills of democratic deliberation—listening carefully, asking which stakeholders were not at the table, identifying the value conflicts underlying disagreements, and weighing trade-offs in policy choices—were applicable in their everyday lives, not just in the political sphere (Harriger, 2014). Further, students didn't have to be part of a 4-year program in order to benefit from deliberative dialogue; indeed, "even limited exposure makes a difference" (Harriger & McMillan, 2007, p. 86).

Many observers are discouraged by contemporary American politics, especially the incivility, hyperpolarization, and inability to work across differences. The Association of American Colleges & Universities National Task Force on Civic Learning and Democratic Engagement (2012) recently described a "civic malaise" in the United States, in which a growing number of Americans are "sideline citizens," who don't vote and lack confidence in and knowledge about their political institutions (pp. 1, 6). Students don't develop democratic capabilities simply by reading about them; they are "honed through hands-on, face-to-face, active engagement in the midst of differing perspectives about how to address common problems that affect the well-being of the nation and the world" (pp. 2–3). The Task Force specifically recommended the methods of intergroup dialogue and deliberative dialogue, which it called "powerful pedagogies that promote civic learning" (p. 55).

I adapted the format for deliberative dialogue suggested by North Carolina Campus Compact to meet the needs of my history course, editing the process to fit it into a 70-minute class meeting but retaining the following 3 key elements:

1. preparatory consideration of three position papers;
2. ground rules for how the dialogue will be conducted; and
3. face-to-face dialogue characterized by broad, open-minded, respectful participation and a format providing equal time given to explore the strengths and weaknesses of each position.

I held a deliberative dialogue session on three separate occasions, each to close a unit of the course. The first dialogue, held less than two weeks into the semester, considered the results of Reconstruction; the second, about halfway through the semester, focused on problems related to the rise of industrial capitalism; and the third, which took place about three-quarters of the way through the semester, grappled with controversies of the 1960s.

Before each dialogue, students read three different position papers, each summarizing a common perspective on a historical problem or situation. Providing at least three positions is important because it discourages participants from falling into two polarized and oversimplified camps. In other venues, organizers of a dialogue might spend weeks talking with all the stakeholders on the issue before creating those position papers. In the interests of efficiency, and because most of the stakeholders on these historical issues were dead, I wrote the position papers. I created three short (one- or two-page) essays for each dialogue, aiming to craft three clear and distinct arguments, making each as persuasive as possible, but expressing them in matter-of-fact, unprovocative language.

For the first dialogue, students were asked to evaluate Reconstruction from their viewpoint in the present day. The position papers made the case for the following three interpretations:

1. Reconstruction was a disappointment because it was a lost opportunity for implementing equality.
2. Reconstruction was a failure because virtually no one was happy by the end of it.
3. Reconstruction was a success, especially given the circumstances.

For the second dialogue, I experimented by asking students to view the problems of the past from the perspective of someone who lived in 1912. I posed the question, "What should we do about industrial capitalism?" and provided three common answers Americans expressed at the time:

1. Leave the system as it is.
2. Use the power of the federal government to make some reforms.
3. Change to a whole different economic system.

For the third dialogue, I reverted to asking students to evaluate the 1960s from their present-day perspective. The "headlines" for the three positions were as follows:

1. The 1960s was a period of dangerous disorder.
2. The 1960s was a great period in which the United States truly and effectively enacted its principles.
3. The 1960s was disappointing because the nation did not go far enough to address its problems.

On the day of the in-class dialogue, students brought notes on each interpretation as their "ticket in the door" to class. Their homework assignment for the first dialogue read:

> The goal for today's deliberative dialogue is for you to understand how different historians might evaluate the period of Reconstruction and to further develop your own perspective on the period. For *each* of the 3 positions, think about what facts you know about Reconstruction and how they impact the ways you agree AND disagree with each position. Come to class with some proof that you've thought about the persuasive and less persuasive aspects of *each* position. That proof could be a bulleted list for each position or a printout of the positions that you've marked all your opinions/comments on.
>
> Now that you've thought carefully about each position, which one would you say most aligns with your evaluation of the period of Reconstruction?

As they arrived, students showed me their notes, so I knew everyone was prepared. They sat in seats arranged in a U so that they could see one another and the front whiteboard. I wrote the short headline for each position on the board and added a + and a – for listing the positive and negative points about each position.

Once all the students had arrived, I explained the process and its connection to our course goals. I then reviewed the ground rules, which I'd also assigned as reading. I adapted these from the resources page of the National Coalition for Dialogue & Deliberation's (2008) website. After the first dialogue, this process took only a few minutes. The handout is represented in Figure 6.1.

Figure 6.1. Ground rules for deliberation.

The point of deliberative dialogue is to gain a deeper and more nuanced understanding of a particular situation or issue and to gain practice in the democratic process of discussing various positions. During our time in class doing "deliberative dialogue," we will spend an equal amount of time on each of the positions. Dr. Festle will be the moderator, but she needs your help for the dialogue to go well. Please make sure you understand our ground rules for deliberation. It is crucial for you to come to class having read and thought about the various positions so that you're ready to participate fully.

- Fairly consider the pros and cons of each option.
- Everyone should feel free to talk, but no one should dominate.
- Keep comments brief so that everyone has a chance to talk.
- One person talks at a time. Please don't cut someone off.
- Stay on topic.
- Listening is as important as talking. Listen carefully and with respect.
- Make sure your messages contribute a unique point or perspective; don't say something someone else already said.
- Speak to each other, not just to the moderator.
- It's okay to disagree, but be sure to show respect for one another. Be willing to respond to questions about your views and ask others to clarify their views.
- Seek to understand rather than persuade. Remember that this is a discussion intended for learning, not a debate.
- Speak for yourself, not as the representative of any group. Remember that others are speaking for themselves, too. Try to avoid overgeneralizing.
- If something someone says hurts or bothers you, say so, and say why.
- Help the facilitator keep things on track.

Then, I officially started the dialogue process by setting a timer for 15 minutes and asking for views about Position 1. My colleague, historian Peter Felten, served as note taker. At first I felt impatient waiting for each new idea to be written on the board, but this waiting provided us with thinking time, and students liked seeing all the points they'd made. I served as moderator for the discussion, prompting students to raise points and counterpoints and to explain further if someone seemed confused. In the beginning students seemed hesitant to disagree, but eventually began doing so in the respectful spirit requested, saying things like, "I don't know; I saw that as a weakness for that position, not a strength because . . ." It's crucial for the moderator to assume a neutral stance. My responsibility was ensuring that the process was conducted conscientiously, in terms of the thoroughness and clarity of the ideas expressed as well as the quality of the interactions between students. The moderator enforces adherence to the ground rules (which proved easy because the students took them seriously) and serves as timekeeper, making sure there is an equal amount of time spent considering each position, including both pros and cons, and letting students know when we were running out of time on a position. I think the structured format lent itself to students having confidence in the fairness of the process; in contrast to some class discussions, in which the quickest or most assertive students or those with the strongest-held views got the most airtime, all students knew there would be equal time to explore each position. Inviting different voices to be heard was another important part of my moderator role. The format created a good opportunity for this goal, too. As time was running out for discussion of one position, there was a chance to ask if anyone who hadn't spoken would like to offer his or her perspective, and when shifting to discussion of the next position, it proved effective to say, "Let's start discussion of this position by hearing from some folks who haven't spoken recently." The combination of ground rules and structure seemed to slow down the students, giving them time to listen, respond to one another, comprehend, look at their notes, and *deliberate*. (It slowed me down, too.)

Because explaining the process and ground rules had taken about 10 minutes, and consideration of the 3 positions took 45 minutes, I had about 10 minutes at the end of class for reflection. I sometimes used a minute or so to make a few observations about themes, commonalities, struggles, or assumptions that the dialogue surfaced, and to thank the students for the quality of their participation. Then for the purposes of articulating their thoughts and getting feedback on the process, I asked the students to respond to the following questions on an index card:

- If you had to advocate one position now, what would it be?
- Has your understanding changed or deepened as a result of this exercise?

This index card, which served as their "ticket out the door," revealed some helpful information. First, all the students were able to take a position. Occasionally a student was less sure ("I am kind of in between Positions 1 and 2"), which illustrated consideration of the alternatives. Although the prompt didn't ask participants to explain *why* they advocated their position, most automatically did so anyway, which was another happy outcome. I found it interesting that I could not have predicted which position many students were going to support, even though they had spoken multiple times in the dialogue. That too suggested that they had taken seriously the request to voice both positive and negative elements of *each* position. For the third dialogue of the semester, I added an additional prompt: "Tell me one thing you agree with from each position." I did this to ensure that students weren't just saying they'd been open-minded in considering the pros and cons of each position; they had to show it. Writing on this prompt took more time, but every student expressed something he or she agreed with in each position. Because my goal was for each student to practice making considered interpretations, this private end-of-class reflection was important.

This reflective writing also provided evidence that the dialogue process had influenced students' thinking. After the first dialogue, 70% of the participants said their understanding had changed or deepened as a result of the exercise; after the second, 85%; and after the third, 86%. Occasionally students said the dialogue had caused them to change their minds from the position they'd advocated before class started. "This exercise . . . helped me rethink my beliefs," reported one. "My understanding has changed quite a bit. Prior to this discussion, I was all for not letting the government interfere, but honestly, it is necessary," said another. A third observed, "As a result of this experience my stance on Position 2 has changed dramatically."

More often, students indicated that their position hadn't drastically changed, but that the exercise was still helpful in understanding perspectives different from their own. "I still believe Recon[struction] was a success," was a fairly typical comment accompanied, "however, I can understand more where the other two positions by were coming from." Similarly, another comment was, "I have a more in-depth and open understanding of the three positions as a whole." A third response echoed that sentiment: "All three sides are more clear now."

Regardless of whether they changed their minds, students often reported that the exercises helped them clarify their thoughts. "It was beneficial because it brought together many of the points I already knew, but had not connected," said one. Another asserted, "My understanding has not changed, but I do now have a better understanding and stronger grasp on what I agree/disagree with and what I believe/support."

Finally, comments revealed that the exercise had deepened their understanding of the issues and time period we were studying. One reported,

"I know more now about Reconstruction. I see views that I didn't think of myself, which I really enjoyed." Another said that he not only learned different present-day perspectives about a time period but also learned about different people in the past: "Now I can think easier from the mind-set of people living in that time period." One student's index card summarized many of the benefits of the dialogue:

> Discussion always deepens my understanding; it is how I learn best. Other people have presented ideas that never crossed my mind, and I can draw upon their ideas to formulate new ones of my own. I feel like I have a greater understanding of the U.S. condition in 1912.

Two other pieces of data may help me evaluate the dialogues. I added supplemental questions to our university's end-of-semester Student Perceptions of Teaching evaluation form. One read, "By practicing in this course I have improved at taking the perspectives of other groups." On a Likert scale of 1 to 6, for which 1 was "strongly disagree" and 6 was "strongly agree," the 5.44 average showed that almost all students agreed or strongly agreed. But because there were other ways we practiced perspective taking over the semester, the rating can't all be attributed to the deliberative dialogues. I added another statement to the evaluation form: "If I had to choose between doing deliberative dialogue and group projects on recent events in U.S. history, I'd choose deliberative dialogues." I asked this because I did have to eliminate a group project in order to add three class days for the dialogues. The average of student responses on this prompt was 4.94. Most students agreed with the statement (75.1% rated it a 5 or 6), but it was certainly not unanimous (a couple of students disagreed fairly strenuously, and a couple were uncertain). Unfortunately, I don't know why they disagreed. In the interests of full disclosure, it's important to mention that the dialogues weren't exciting. I know they weren't as energetic or fun as a team game I designed in which students made strategic decisions while assuming the roles of strikers and factory owners competing for power.

The deliberative dialogue format has great potential for other types of classes. It is especially useful for situations in which students are considering multiple courses of action (such as policy recommendations, treatment decisions, resource allocations, research strategies, or business plans) and when students need practice with seeing the world from different perspectives. The format—with its assurance that minority perspectives receive thorough consideration—is especially useful with sensitive or controversial issues. The format is also adaptable in terms of time (more time or perhaps less might work, depending on the complexity of the issue). In other contexts, as with more advanced students, I could envision having students create the ground rules or research and write the position papers. I know that I will continue to experiment, such as with whether it's more meaningful to have students view the various positions from the perspective of the past or the present, and with ways to debrief the discussion. I want to improve at surfacing the values, priorities, or assumptions that underlie the various positions. Because our third dialogue seemed better than the previous ones, I suspect that familiarity and practice make both participants and moderators more comfortable with the format.

I will definitely use deliberative dialogues in the future. Students reported they'd learned, and I witnessed that during and after the discussion. For the topic of Reconstruction, which is especially important because it sets patterns early in the semester, the dialogue was a significant improvement in achieving my unit objectives. My previous method had been to lecture about three different historians' interpretations and then ask students to do a one-minute free write about which interpretation was most persuasive to them. The deliberative dialogue meant students were more fully engaged and considered each position more thoroughly. Sometimes the dialogues also helped me realize where students didn't understand certain material as well as I'd hoped. Overall, the format helped me meet the three challenges I face related to making thoughtful interpretations about the past, helping students understand differing perspectives, and facilitating more engaging and in-depth group discussions.

Historians make judgments about the past after a thorough, careful process of grappling with multiple types of evidence, evenhandedly examining the experiences of as many people as possible, and carefully reasoning about various interpretations and their implications, and they do so in conversation with others. On a smaller scale, students in an introductory history course can do the same thing through deliberative dialogue. The process provides practice using lifelong skills, values, and dispositions that may develop a more respectful and capable citizenry. It's worth a try!

References

Deardorff, D. K. (2011). Assessing intercultural competence. *New Directions for Institutional Research, 2011*(149), 65–79. doi:10.1002/ir.381

Harriger, K. J. (2014). Deliberative dialogue and the development of democratic dispositions. *New Directions for Higher Education, 2014*(166), 53–61. doi:10.1002/he.20095

Harriger, K. J., & McMillan, J. J. (2007). *Speaking of politics: Preparing college students for democratic citizenship through deliberative dialogue.* Dayton, OH: Charles F. Kettering Foundation.

National Coalition for Dialogue & Deliberation. (2008). *Sample ground rules for D&D processes.* Retrieved from http://ncdd.org/rc/item/1505

National Coalition for Dialogue & Deliberation. (2014). *Engagement streams framework* [Guide]. Retrieved from http://www.ncdd.org/files/rc/2014_Engagement _Streams_Guide_Web.pdf

National Task Force on Civic Learning and Democratic Engagement. (2012). *A crucible moment: College learning democracy's future.* Washington, DC: Association of American Colleges & Universities.

North Carolina Campus Compact. (n.d.). *Deliberative dialogue* [Training handout]. Retrieved from http://www.elon.edu/e-web/org/nccc/DeliberativeDialogue .xhtml

HOW COTEACHING AND OTHER STRATEGIES PROMOTE LIVELY STUDENT ENGAGEMENT

Matthea Marquart and Mary Ann Drury

The Teaching Challenge

In fall 2014, the authors of this chapter came together to plan a new online course for Columbia University's School of Social Work (CSSW) as part of the Master of Science in Social Work (MSSW) program. The course—Staff Development, Training, and Coaching—was piloted in spring 2015 as one of Columbia's first online courses. Mary Ann Drury was the instructor, and Matthea Marquart was the teaching assistant (TA).

Our online course focused on teaching students how to design and implement innovative learning programs to enhance professional development for human services employees. This meant that we needed to design and implement a particularly innovative learning program ourselves. The course was a seven-week elective that attracted students interested in careers in learning and employee development. When Drury taught the course residentially in the past without a TA, students were highly engaged, and we wanted to maintain that level of engagement in the online environment.

We anticipated that our greatest challenge online would be to draw all students into lively discussions of the content throughout the course, especially large whole-class virtual discussions. Live online classes carry a high risk of students disengaging due to the multiple distractions available online. We wanted our students to be present and participate in the kind of meaningful discussions that would enable them to meet the learning objectives.

As experienced instructors and social workers, we were familiar with the many opportunities to establish powerful relationships with students in the residential classroom, and we wanted to capture the excitement of live group discussions and respond effectively to group dynamics online. Prior informal discussions with students confirmed that they shared similar concerns. Although we had high enrollment for our initial course, most students chose the online class for convenience rather than any strong preference for learning online. We accepted these challenges as opportunities to be inventive.

Our First Strategy: Coteach

A key element of our strategy was to partner closely to create an environment that supported animated discussions and stimulating content exploration. Despite Drury's strong subject matter expertise gained from 25 years of industry experience and 7 years teaching graduate-level social work, this was her first foray into online teaching. Fortunately, CSSW pairs online instructors with TAs, and Marquart brought more than 10 years of experience in online teaching and training. We agreed that our partnership should leverage our mutual strengths.

As colleagues at Columbia, we took advantage of our ability to be physically present in the same location for our class sessions by sitting together in a conference room and sharing one mic and webcam throughout the course. In the few minutes before we were scheduled to meet with our students live, we had the spontaneous idea to model ourselves after public television coanchors Judy Woodruff and Gwen Ifill, respected public figures who offer news updates, share thought-provoking analyses, and ask guests provocative questions. We emulated their conversational dialogue in an intellectually demanding atmosphere of analysis and inquiry.

We found that coteaching offered certain advantages. We could model active participation and interpersonal interaction for students. We shared our differences of opinion or unique perspectives about the material and encouraged our students to do the same. Together we had extemporaneous dialogues about the content, and we took turns leading parts of the classes. This approach modeled for students that having different views and interpretations of the content was okay while increasing the energy level of the classes and providing entertainment value that heightened student attentiveness, all of which encouraged participation.

To establish rapport with our class, we occasionally disclosed personal anecdotes or workplace experiences that were relevant to the course content.

Sharing our stories encouraged students to open up about their previous experiences in field settings or employment and brought the material to life. In addition, our stories deepened our interpersonal connections with the students. As an example, Marquart once shared an anecdote about a family member's workplace experience that perfectly illustrated the concept Drury was reviewing on a slide. This ignited meaningful responses from several students who came on the webcam to share their work experiences and changes in their thinking about these past events based on what they were learning in class.

Our Second Strategy: Provide Clear Expectations, Support, and Options for Participation

Effective discussions take place in an environment in which students feel safe enough to take risks and share their thoughts, ideas, questions, and concerns about the content. Knowing that many students can be initially shy about speaking up online, we sought ways to help students overcome anxiety and self-consciousness around appearing on camera. We followed standard good practices for engaging students, such as using student names and expressing verbal and nonverbal interest in comments. We offered continuous support through multiple invitations, encouragement, and enthusiastic interest and appreciation for student efforts and commentary. We communicated high expectations for participation, but we balanced that demand with sensitivity and empathy toward student anxieties about speaking on webcam. This included offering them the option to participate in whole-class discussions via webcam or typed chat.

Initially, giving students a choice in how to participate gave them a sense of greater control. Nonetheless, we gradually pushed reluctant students to participate outside of their comfort zone. We reminded them that public speaking is both a common anxiety and a critical workplace skill, and that this was an ideal supportive learning space in which to experiment and practice developing proficiency. As part of this practice, one of our first assignments was to post a one-minute introductory video in a discussion forum. For this assignment, we gave students technical tips on how to create a successful video, model videos we created, and four questions to answer:

1. Where are you from?
2. What is your field placement this semester?
3. Why are you taking this course?

4. What topic(s) in this course are you most interested in learning about (e.g., learning organizations, types of knowledge transfer, coaching, mentoring, etc.)?

This preclass assignment helped students overcome some of their initial anxiety about being on camera by giving them a chance to try it in a non-threatening setting that they controlled.

We also supported and encouraged students to take the risk of participating in whole-class discussions by preparing them step-by-step. During class, we eased them into discussions by polling their opinions and requiring all of them to participate. Viewing other classmates' opinions created a sense of community and stimulated their desire to share additional thoughts. Then we asked for volunteers to come the webcam to elaborate on their perspective. Students could also contribute by typing into a live chat. This process allowed them to add more deeply to the discussion and underscored that every student had the potential to participate.

Another way that we prepared students to participate was by sharing a selection of publicly posted opinions from the discussion forum homework to jump-start whole-class discussions. Prior to class, we e-mailed students whose posts were selected so that they could prepare to kick off the discussion.

We rewarded students and held them accountable for their participation using a class participation grading rubric for each week's class session. The rubric, shown in Table 7.1, included points for participating in polls, in chat, and on webcam. We used it to provide specific targeted feedback about the *quality* of each student's participation. This included recognition for positive participation, recommendations for making improvements, and encouragement. When a student's grades indicated deficient participation, the student either independently changed the relevant behavior in order to achieve the desired points or requested individual coaching on how to make improvements.

For some, the rubric was controversial. We received selected feedback that grading student participation undermined its meaningfulness because some students were contributing simply to get the desired grade. However, their changed behavior included active participation in all of our discussions, which was a desirable outcome.

We offered to be available either immediately after class on webcam or by phone appointment to consult with individual students on how to overcome any personal barriers to active participation. For example, one international student expressed concern about the efficacy of her English language speaking skills; we made a recommendation that she found acceptable and that led to improvements.

TABLE 7.1
Sample Grading Rubric for Live Online Class Participation

Component	Description
Intro	**Why Participation Matters:** High-quality participation is valued because it contributes to the learning environment and supports a collaborative, engaged, and respectful classroom atmosphere. It also provides valuable feedback to the instructor(s) and supports our ability to understand, evaluate, and respond to the ongoing learning needs of students. The following represents full participation: • On-time arrival and ready to participate • Present in session throughout (excluding any class breaks) • Chats • Polls • Contributions in breakout sessions • Responses to instructor requests (e.g., key takeaways) • Webcam use on at least three occasions over seven weeks
Points	**Participation and Attendance Criteria**
10	**Meets expectations with exemplary participation:** You went beyond what I consider "satisfactory participation" as detailed in the following and made a significant contribution to the live session that positively impacted the discussion of the topics. This contribution might come by way of sharing an opinion, introducing new material, raising a question, relating course content to a personal experience, or many other methods of participation. You attended the live session in a timely manner.
9	**Meets expectations with exemplary participation, with a few minor exceptions:** With the exception of one or two instances, you made a significant contribution to the live session that positively impacted the discussion of the topics. This contribution might come by way of sharing an opinion, introducing new material, raising a question, relating course content to a personal experience, or many other methods of participation. You attended the live session in a timely manner. Examples of the difference between a 10 and a 9 score might be your willingness to appear on webcam, share your small-group findings, or otherwise lead your peers in their understanding and acquisition of new knowledge during the live session.

(Continues)

Table 7.1 (*Continued*)

Points	Participation and Attendance Criteria
8	**Nearly meets expectations with satisfactory participation:** You were prepared, engaged, and contributed to the live session. You were thoughtful and considerate in your responses when prompted and demonstrated that you had completed the weekly assignments.
7	**Nearly meets expectations with satisfactory participation, with slight reservations:** With the exception of one or two instances, you were generally prepared, engaged, and contributed to the live session. For the most part, you were thoughtful and considerate in your responses when prompted and demonstrated that you had completed the weekly assignments. You attended the live session in a timely manner.
5	**Partially meets expectations with minimal participation:** You logged on and remained present for the duration of the live session. You participated minimally and/or the quality of your participation did not meet the criteria for satisfactory participation. You attended the live session in a timely manner.
3	**Barely meets expectations with minimal participation:** You logged on and remained present for the duration of the live session. You participated minimally and/or you were late arriving or not present for the entire live session.
0	**Does not meet expectations:** You did not participate or you did not attend the live session and failed to notify me that you would not be in attendance.

Our Third Strategy: Create Detailed Plans With Opportunities for Spontaneity

Every weekend, we met to create a detailed class plan for the coming week. The plan served to keep us on time, led to our feeling and looking confident and capable, and ensured that we covered the required material. Table 7.2 shows a sample plan.

Creating such detailed plans also enabled us to prepare for how to respond to any online technical glitches. These were thankfully rare, but handling interruptions with confidence afforded another opportunity

TABLE 7.2
Sample Plan for Live Online Class (Week 4)

Component	Allotted Time
Slide 1: Welcome to Module 4	1 minute
Slide 2: Announcements • Tech update • Comment on grading rubric • Halfway through course: Alert! • Student suggestion	2 minutes
Slide 3: Module 4 Overview: Mention Work Due • Readings • Discussion Forum: Sample Online Training • Part 1 Needs Assessment: Final Assignment	1 minute
Slide 4: Integrating Readings Into Discussion • Today we will be more active about integrating readings into class discussion • YouTube clip: "Why Work Doesn't Happen at Work" • Try to integrate something interesting you learned from reading when you share	1 minute
Slides 5–7: Debrief Discussion Forum • 5: Discussion Forum: Sample Online Training (two seconds to introduce topic) • 6: Broadcast their responses "Liked" or "Did Not Like." Be brief! • 7: Why effective or not?	3 minutes
Slide 8: Invite four students (webcam) to briefly elaborate • Go to next slide: opportunity to review required reading	7 minutes
IT IS NOW 7:15	
Slides 9–12: Case study • 9: Best practices for online training. Marquart talks about the case and best practices • 10: Transfer of training—three key factors. Marquart refers to slide content: invite two students to apply the case (webcam) • 11: Kirkpatrick's four levels of evaluation model. Marquart refers to slide content: invite two students to apply the case (webcam) • 12: Key takeaways from Module 3 content (Feedback). Drury refers to content: invite two students to apply the case (webcam)	15 minutes

(Continues)

Table 7.2 (*Continued*)

Component	Allotted Time
IT IS NOW 7:30	
Slide 13: Definition of *risk* and risk *management*	1 minute
Slide 14: Internal versus external risk Brief: Ask students to name two risks that were addressed in case study Type brief responses into chat (one- to four-word description of risk) Marquart comment on: • Scalable training • Support expansion • Financial and logistical training	2 minutes
Slide 15: TED Talk: view one minute, then breakout groups	22 minutes
Debrief with the spokesperson from each group on webcam together	5 minutes
IT IS NOW 8:00	
Slide 16: One-minute break: show video about the importance of walking and move around	1 minute
Slides 17–19 • 17: Why manage risk? • 18: Managing risk using training • 19: Rationale for training	6 minutes
Slide 20: • Ask students why many organizations resist training managers • Students type responses into chat	3 minutes
IT IS NOW 8:10	
Slides 21–25: Case study: Hurricane Sandy (Drury) • Students chat while Drury talks about case; make this an interactive conversation	15 minutes
IT IS NOW 8:25	
Slide 26: Student feedback on course learning outcomes Polls: 1. Is this course helping you meet these learning outcomes? 2. If yes, what has been helpful? 3. If no, what suggestions do you have for us? Time for student questions and feedback	5 minutes
THE END	

to model professionalism and comfort with the online platform, even if we weren't necessarily feeling that way. Our apparent calmness helped lower the student anxiety that can hinder participation.

We also planned moments with the potential for spontaneity. As an example, during our first class, our plan included a two-minute stretch exercise at the one-hour mark. For this exercise, we stood up from our chairs and joined in the exercise with our students, which created a fun, shared interactive experience and some unexpected levity. Seeing us in human moments like this may have relaxed students during class.

Assessing the Impact of Our Strategies

Each week, we informally assessed the effectiveness of our strategies. For example, students' participation grades reflected how well they were meeting participation expectations as defined in the participation rubric. With one exception, these grades rose over the course of the semester, indicating that most students were gradually participating more fully in class discussions.

Our webinar support specialist also furnished assessment data. Our specialist attended each class session to provide back-end platform support and rapid resolution of any technical difficulties, as well as a written report after each class with participation data such as the class's prediscussion poll responses and counts of each student's contribution in chat discussions. These reports proved invaluable in tracking student engagement and showed improving student and instructor performance over time.

In addition, our students supplied important feedback. At the end of each class, we asked them to share their key takeaways and evaluate particular activities in short-answer polls. This gave us a window into their thinking, promoted student reflection on their learning, and served as a formative assessment. Their weekly takeaways documented that they were meeting course learning objectives, and their weekly feedback about the whole-class discussions and coteaching model was overwhelmingly positive. During the final class session, we conducted cumulative anonymous polls to gather ideas for making improvements to future classes. Table 7.3 displays some response counts.

Many students expressed their appreciation for our coteaching style. They enjoyed our interactions around the material, our conversational yet respectful tone, our transparent sharing of workplace experiences, and our occasional informal banter. They pointed out that this unique style both modeled and communicated a powerful invitation to join in on the discussion.

Another informal source of feedback was the positive social buzz among students about our course. This created welcomed press for CSSW's new online courses, which increased future enrollment. Much to our delight,

TABLE 7.3

Student Feedback in Anonymous Polls During the Final Class Session

Poll Question	Student Responses
Did the chat feature help you engage and connect with one another?	18 responses • Yes: 83.3% • No: 16.7%
Did the chat feature help you engage and connect with the instructor?	18 responses • Yes: 94.4% • No: 5.6%
Were you only incentivized to complete the assignments when points were awarded?	18 responses • Yes: 44.4% • No: 55.6%
Do you need extra encouragement to come on webcam?	17 responses • Yes: 52.9% • No: 47.1%

many of our students were won over to the online learning experience and subsequently became involved in CSSW's online campus. Out of our 18 students, 1 became an online learning ambassador recruiting new students, 2 became online TAs, 1 became a webinar support specialist for online courses, and 1 will be a virtual guest speaker in online classes.

To our surprise, student participation in the online classroom had a more intimate and honest quality overall than we had experienced in residential courses. Our students gradually became comfortable and willing to take risks when sharing their content-relevant thoughts and opinions. We believe that the online class culture of active participation and instructor transparency that we strove to create was a strong contributing factor.

Advice for Other Faculty

We offer our colleagues the following five strategies for actively engaging students and enhancing their participation in the online classroom:

1. Experiment with a coteaching model by partnering with a TA or by mentoring an instructor who is new to online teaching. Consider how you will play to one another's complementary strengths during the live sessions. Ideally, your relationship will model interest, excitement, and mutual respect. Although we carefully scripted each class agenda beforehand, we made room for natural, spontaneous exchanges. This lent an

element of uncertainty or risk and sparked a bit of excitement for us as well as the students. They enjoyed the opportunity to hear us discuss course content in relaxed, conversational tones and were eager to join in on the conversation.

2. Establish and communicate norms and expectations for full and meaningful participation. Take a few moments at the start of the course to emphasize the value and importance of active student participation. A participation grading rubric will provide continuous feedback and encourage and support ongoing student involvement. Communicate your hopes for creating a culture of frank, energetic, and valuable student-instructor interaction.

3. Find ways to share and highlight interesting student contributions in the live classroom. Students enjoy seeing their opinions publicly featured on slides. It lets them know that you read and value their work and consider it worthy of sharing with others.

4. Ask students to type their key takeaways into a public poll at the end of each class. This exercise quickly provides a wealth of information, helps you assess whether students are on track toward meeting the learning objectives, and validates the importance of their feedback and participation.

5. Create opportunities to interact with students outside of the online classroom. One-on-one meetings strengthen relationships, deepen student-teacher interaction, and indicate that you are invested in your students.

8

GOT INTROVERTS? GET CAE (COLLABORATIVE AUTOETHNOGRAPHY)

Mary Shapiro

We've all had those two or three students each semester who never talk. Even with the "threat" of 30% of their grade depending on class participation, they remain silent. Now imagine teaching a course with not just a *few* quiet students, but *all 25 students* are those silent, stone-faced, contemplative learners.

Starting in the fall of 2015, Simmons College, a small women's-centered liberal arts school in Boston, rolled out a new general education curriculum. This curriculum, spanning all four years of an undergraduate's tenure, was designed to be distinctive, better prepare students for the world postgraduation, and develop students' leadership capacity. Simmons students are now required to take a leadership course in their second semester of their first year. Faculty across the campus were invited to develop a leadership course that sprang from their own discipline, research, or passion and create content around specified learning objectives, namely, diversity and inclusion, teams, public speaking, and leadership.

More than 20 courses were created. One investigated how television frames different social identities. Another examined the lives and motivations of four protagonists who chose to challenge U.S. laws in suits that reached the Supreme Court. Still another looked at comedy and how it is used to speak truth to power. I chose to pursue my passion of enabling introverts to see themselves as leaders and build a course where self-identified introverts would challenge the conventional extroverted definition of *leadership*, recognize the value their introverted style offers, and develop skills and strategies to lead from their strengths. I had to use a pedagogy that would not only prevent 60 contact hours of "crickets" but also 60 hours of the dead-air hush of a crypt.

In this new course, Leading Quietly in a World That Celebrates Extroversion, students read Susan Cain's (2013) text of almost the same title, *Quiet: The Power of Introverts in a World That Can't Stop Talking*. The first third of the course challenged most introverts' lifelong feedback that they were "too quiet/shy/slow/bookish to be a leader." Through appreciative inquiry exercises, my introverts uncovered their behaviors that other people appreciated and the value that those behaviors had previously produced in teams, communities, and relationships. Students discovered that they had indeed already enacted leadership, often in nonextroverted but very powerful ways. During the middle of the course, students progressed through a series of exercises that iteratively imposed multiple lenses over basic definitions of *leadership*. These activities enabled students to access and then evaluate the messages they had received about leadership growing up—first as introverts, second as women, third by race/ethnicity, and fourth by other identities of their choice. The final outcome of the semester was their personal leader profile and an analysis of their life's journey that created that profile.

I intentionally designed the course to capitalize on the introvert's likely attributes of deep analytic and critical thinking with lots of reading and reflection, but I still needed to get students to *talk*! Leadership, after all, implies relationships with others. Discourse would not only improve the rigor of their own thinking but also develop their relational leadership skills—and make the class more fun.

Strategy Employed

I used many "cricket-avoiding" pedagogies during class discussions, and I relied most on the pedagogy called collaborative autoethnography (CAE). It is an iterative research process that promotes deep reflective thinking in six stages:

1. Individuals who want to collectively explore a particular social phenomenon form a research team and generate an initial set of questions.
2. Individuals first write privately in response to those prompts.
3. They then share their reflections with the group, which then collectively identifies common similarities, differences, and themes.
4. Those themes become the next prompts for further individual reflection, often deepened with readings.
5. The cycle of sharing continues until it exhausts that lens (no new discoveries or time runs out).
6. The group or each individual writes about their findings, often building models to explain the phenomenon explored.

In our culture, the scientific method of stating a hypothesis, gathering data, and analyzing data to either support or reject the hypothesis is so dominant that it is taken for granted as the only way of knowing and meaning making. More recently, new methodologies have emerged. One of these is autoethnography (AE), in which the sample and the researcher fuse together, the data are stories from the researcher's own experiences, and the goal of the analyses is not to prove/disprove hypotheses but to develop a model that explains some social phenomenon. For example, you may want to explore what impact being the daughter of first-generation immigrants has had on your career choices. Although the data are personal stories, AE is different from writing an autobiography. Autobiography captures your personal stories. *Auto*, self, *ethnography*, the study of culture, goes beyond personal stories by analyzing them in the larger relational and societal context. AE provides a lens through which you examine those contexts over time and seek to understand how they have shaped you into who you are today. By identifying the social dynamics that have surrounded you and identifying your reaction to and interaction with them, AE enables you to uncover the foundation of the beliefs and perspectives you hold today. With CAE, the sample increases to include multiple individuals, and the data grow as we accumulate and share our stories. Our analyses then become an iterative process of self-reflection followed by group discussion, which can lead to further self-reflection and subsequent group discussion.

My students used CAE to explore their multiple social identities and how those identities informed their definitions of and aspirations for leadership. This process recognized that over our lives we accumulate and internalize social messages promulgated by our parents, teachers, partners, employers, the media, laws, and social policy. Those messages tell us how we as individuals are expected to act and to lead. Without introspection and reflection, our personal identity is an amalgamation of the external messages we have received. With introspection and reflection, we can challenge those messages and craft our own identity (as a woman, as a woman of color, as a leader, etc.).

Often used to examine social phenomena such as the impact of religion on political agendas or community policing on racism, CAE also has been used to examine social movements, organizational culture and change, and education policy, among other phenomena. Regardless of your topic, CAE generates two beneficial outcomes:

1. CAE prepares *all* students to participate in classroom discussions by giving them time to prepare their responses ahead of time. This is particularly important for quieter or more contemplative students. Rather than asking a question in real time and pausing to give those students more

time to build their verbal response, CAE essentially poses the questions hours or days in advance.

2. CAE also engenders deeper classroom conversations in a number of ways. Because all students (including the spontaneous speakers) are given prompts and time to prepare, their comments are grounded in deeper thinking. With each cycle of sharing individual reflections and identifying themes, the classroom discussion moves from sharing and understanding to collaboratively analyzing, synthesizing, and evaluating the topic.

The Process

To perform CAE, I used the following six-step process:

1. Build trust.
2. Set up boundaries, expectations, and rules of engagement.
3. Collect data.
4. Analyze data.
5. Interpret data.
6. Write.

Because of the intimate nature of the data, individuals' personal stories, it was essential in the first step to build trust in the classroom. This was even more critical for introverts, who naturally keep personal information private, and because of the difficult conversations we'd be having around gender, race, class, and ethnicity. The first five classes of the semester were devoted to appreciative inquiry, where students collected and shared positive experiences and supportive examples of their leadership.

Concurrent with Step 1, we regularly reviewed how we were working together in Step 2 by setting boundaries, expectations, and rules of engagement. Through those conversations, we determined the aspirational culture we wanted in our classroom; that is, how we wanted to feel working together, and our expectations for each other's behaviors. Not surprisingly, confidentiality was a big concern. Each student was essentially a human subject. Not only did we agree that we would keep our stories and our identities confidential, but students also had the option of using pseudonyms to protect the identities of people *in* their stories.

Another norm revolved around identity politics, an additional CAE challenge (Klinker & Todd, 2007). As a class we resolved to remind ourselves and each other that these were personal stories, lived and experienced individually, and not representative of the larger social identity groups to which we belonged.

The third step was to collect data. Stories are CAE data, and the more detailed, the better. In response to a prompt (e.g., "Recall a time when you . . ."), stories could come from the students' own memories; interviews with others; or archival data from Facebook, Pinterest pages, and diaries. To elicit more details and encourage deeper thinking, students first wrote their stories in journals on our educational learning platform (Moodle). All students had their own journals that I could read and respond to privately with additional questions to further their exploration before class.

Often student reflection was primed by readings or by previous class discussions. This varied prompt by prompt. Sometimes I wanted to capture their spontaneous responses as a baseline, uninfluenced by scholarly models. Other times I wanted to give them ideas of what to look for in their histories or draw out their own examples of concepts like gendered norms. In CAE, it is useful to think of Step 3 (collect data) and Step 4 (analyze data) as iterative steps. As we listened to our first collection of stories, we analyzed them to the extent that we identified "recurring topics, unique details, emerging patterns" (Chang, Ngunjiri, & Hernandez, 2013, p. 103). We also assessed where to delve deeper or whether we had collected sufficient data for that topic. That analysis would then lead students to further data collection as they went back in their life experiences to once again seek out new stories or further details. The ultimate goal of these data analyses was to identify themes. I initiated prompts that would set the discussion in new directions, and the class also developed prompts. For example, I initiated the prompt, "Recall a time when you acted as an extrovert. Why did you do that? What did you do? What were the outcomes?" Two themes emerged in student responses: "I was passionate about it" or "The job required it." Students then crafted the next prompt to recall times when they were forced to be an extrovert as a comparison for more fully understanding their emotional responses and motivators.

Data analysis (Step 4) was conducted in two stages. First, students shared their stories in trios. These trios both allowed airtime for every story, which would not have been possible in a class of 25, and, very importantly, furnished a more intimate space for introverts to begin sharing and analyzing. I assembled these trios in advance based on students' answers to two questions: "What social identities are most salient to you?" and "What social identities are you most interested in learning more about?" I then grouped students to connect the identities they brought and the identities they sought. In these trios, which remained stable through the semester (another nod to introverts), students listened to each other's stories, asked questions to uncover further details, and did their first draft of theme building.

Trios shared their themes with the rest of the class with the goal of creating a manageable number of differentiated themes. For example, a broad theme (e.g., birth order) would be teased out into more specific themes (e.g., demands made by older siblings, less face time with Mom). Students could then see elements of their own stories distributed across the themes. Step 5 was to interpret data. Throughout all our conversations we wrestled with the question, "What does this all mean?" Questions such as, "In what ways did contextual factors (cultural, social, economic) impact your experiences?" or "How might your stories have been different had you made different choices?" enabled students to make sense of their own experiences. Step 6, the final step, was to write. To summarize their learning, students wrote a final paper capturing their own process of leader identity. Using their own stories, the collaboratively developed themes, and the extant literature as the data, they constructed a visual model of their leader identity journey along with supporting text that captured how they defined themselves as leaders today and what life experiences, messages, and decisions had brought them to that point.

Tweaking the Crickets

Although CAE embeds many cricket-preventing components (e.g., long lead times to craft responses to questions, individual sharing in stable small groups), I still encountered 25 pairs of eyeballs staring at me like deer in headlights when I first asked trios to report out their themes. The previously boisterous conversations became radio silence when I asked them to share in the full group. After some floundering on my part, I adjusted the process in two ways:

1. *Reporting out*: As part of the small-group discussion process, trios needed to summarize their themes for the verbal report out. To avoid the most extroverted introvert becoming the spokesperson, trios rotated the role of the reporter.
2. *Full-group theme-making*: We often did a gallery walk as the first step of theme-making as a full group. Trios wrote their themes on the whiteboards around the room. After the verbal report out, students had time to walk around and read all the themes. That extra time for thinking kick-started the class discussion of observations and suggestions.

Evaluation

My informal evaluations assessed the level of student participation and the depth of the discussion. Regarding the former, over the semester I charted student participation per class and found that most students contributed consistently at least once every 2 class periods, not counting talking in trios. This also enabled me to intervene with silent students and help them strategize contributing in future classes. Two of the 25 students would not voluntarily contribute; with a heads up that I would do so, I cold-called on them. Participation increased to 100%! Hooray! Additionally, student feedback on the online evaluations gave the course high scores on "freedom to ask questions and express opinions" (100% agreed) and "inclusive learning environment" (94% agreed). In the open comment section, multiple students expressed appreciation for the discussion process in general and the "intelligent and respectful conversations in a safe environment" specifically.

Evidence of the depth of discussion came from two sources: students' journals, which prepared them for class discussions, and their final papers, which reflected class discussions. The rigor of their journal reflections counted as 8% of their semester grade. After reading all students' entries for a particular prompt, I assigned each student points based on the level of detail in his or her personal stories (data) and his or her analyses of those stories. About a quarter of the students were highly reflective from the beginning, and half increased their rigor over time as they learned my expectations from my questions back to them. Only a few journals remained minimal and shallow. Interestingly, the level of rigor in their journals did not predict who tended to contribute in class. Like all students, introverts or not, some were more reflective introspectively, whereas others framed their thoughts in real time during class discussions.

I graded the final papers on the following two traits:

1. The leader profile is personal, compelling, and reflective of the many data sources upon which it draws.
2. The leader identity development story is compelling, draws upon multiple incidents, and reveals significant introspection and reflection. Conclusions and insights are well supported by life experiences.

The paper was worth 30 points of the semester grade, and 30% of those points were based on the rigor deduced from the preceding traits. Class discussions very powerfully advanced students' thinking about their own leadership journey, and not surprisingly, the students' grades were high. In many papers, students wrote about their shock and validation in hearing other student experiences that mirrored their own.

Outcomes

I have only completed the first semester using CAE, and we all know that it takes multiple times teaching to get it right. Through the semester I adjusted the process to make it work more effectively and will continue to do so. But reading students' final papers powerfully revealed the extent to which students transformed from believing themselves to be passive, unempowered followers to being engaged leaders. One student captured that transition using a quote in the following:

> Edith Wharton says, "There are two ways of spreading light: to be the candle or the mirror that reflects it." I see the mirror as the introverts and quiet leaders of the world and the candle as the extroverts. . . . Introverts are an essential part of society that offers another side of life that we may not see without them.

Closing Thoughts

By using CAE in a class of 25 introverts, I was able to get them thinking and get them talking. CAE enabled students to examine the socialized messages about leadership they'd received over their lives through multiple vehicles (relationships, media, politics) and pertaining to multiple identities (culture, gender, race, ethnicity, sexual orientation). Then they could decide which messages to reject or act on in the future. I encourage instructors to consider using this pedagogy to examine any social, individual, or organizational phenomenon; to transform student thinking by uncovering their underlying assumptions, biases, and beliefs; or to generate an informed platform on which to make future decisions. For more guidance, consider Custer (2014); Jones, Adams, and Ellis (2013); Ngunjiri, Hernandez, and Chang (2010); Tedlock (2000); and Wall (2006).

References

Cain, S. (2013). *Quiet: The power of introverts in a world that can't stop talking.* New York, NY: Random House.

Chang, H., Ngunjiri, F. W., & Hernandez, K. C. (2013). *Collaborative autoethnography.* Walnut Creek, CA: Left Coast Press.

Custer, D. (2014). Autoethnography as a transformative research method. *The Qualitative Report, 19,* 1–13. Retrieved from http://www.nova.edu/ssss/QR/QR19/custer21.pdf

Jones, S. H., Adams, T. E., & Ellis C. (Eds.). (2013). *Handbook of autoethnography.* Walnut Creek, CA: Left Coast Press.

Klinker, J. F., & Todd, R. H. (2007). Two autoethnographies: A search for understanding of gender and age. *The Qualitative Report, 12*(2), 166–183. Retrieved from http://www.nova.edu/ssss/QR/QR12-2/klinker.pdf

Ngunjiri, F. W., Hernandez, K. C., & Chang, H. (2010). Living autoethnography: Connecting life and research. *Journal of Research Practice, 6*(1), Article E1.

Tedlock, B. (2000). Ethnography and ethnographic representation. In N. K. Denzin & Y. S. Lincoln (Eds.), *Handbook of qualitative research* (pp. 455–486). Thousand Oaks, CA: Sage.

Wall, S. (2006). An autoethnography on learning about autoethnography. *International Journal of Qualitative Methods, 5*(2), article 9. Retrieved from https://www.ualberta.ca/~iiqm/backissues/5_2/PDF/wall.pdf

9

USING A CONTEMPLATIVE PEDAGOGY TO PROMOTE DISCUSSION IN A FIRST-YEAR SEMINAR

Jennifer W. Shewmaker

My classrooms are active learning environments. One of the keys to successful active learning experiences is student participation. Having taught at the university level for the past 14 years, I thought I understood how to stimulate engaging discussions with my students. However, once I agreed to teach a first-year student seminar 2 years ago, I realized that I was facing a new challenge. The seminar, called Cornerstone, is the first course within the university's liberal arts core. Cornerstone examines ways of thinking across the disciplines, using challenging, global issues to build student skill in thinking in critical, global, and mission-oriented ways. The goal is to prepare students to make a difference in the world. As a part of this course, students have opportunities to explore complex topics, such as the banality of evil, living with mindfulness, engaging culture critically, and global thinking. I found that even though the students seemed interested in the topics, they struggled to engage in class discussion.

Knowing that this might be the case for first-year students, when I taught the course the first time, I used concepts from the book *How Learning Works* (Ambrose, Bridges, DiPietro, Lovett, & Norman, 2010) to try to craft engaging prompts and introductory activities that would connect with the students' previous experience. However, we still endured many moments of long silences with students unwilling, or perhaps unable, to speak up. Often, those who had not spoken up in the discussion stayed after class to talk with me about the prompt. This led me to believe that the students were generally interested in the issues being discussed, but something was getting in the way of their participation.

In the second year of teaching the course, I decided to focus on the strategies that the research suggests for increasing the value that students place on course activities—two tactics, in particular: connecting the material to students' interests and providing authentic, real-world connections (Ambrose et al., 2010). In order to do this, I began to think about how I might help students relate the core course concepts to their concerns. I also wanted to provide opportunities for them to make relevant, real-world associations with the sophisticated ideas that we were discussing. Because my prepared prompts had not been completely successful in doing this, I knew that I needed to add another strategy. So I implemented an approach focused on using the contemplative pedagogy of informal writing.

As a member of the Association for Contemplative Mind in Higher Education (ACMHE) and a contemplative pedagogy learning community at my university, I had been considering for the previous few years how contemplative pedagogies might be effectively incorporated into college courses to give students a better learning experience. Using resources and sample syllabi from the ACMHE, I identified informal writing as a practice that would fit well into the structure of Cornerstone. Educational research has supported its effectiveness in promoting positive learning outcomes and the achievement of learning goals (Hudd, Smart, & Delohery, 2011; Petko, Egger, & Graber, 2014).

I incorporated informal writing into daily practice with two goals in mind. First, I wanted to give students the chance to practice mindfulness and move into being fully present with the course material. Since the questions and ideas that we were discussing were complex, it seemed to be difficult for the first-year students to come into a 10:00 a.m. class in the middle of their busy day and be ready to dive into these topics. Second, I wanted to let students formulate a response to the discussion topic before having to share it with others. Studies have shown that writing before class discussion increases students' sense of preparedness for the activity (Ewell & Rodgers, 2014) and that the combination of writing and discussion in active learning classrooms improves their grades (Linton, Pangle, Wyatt, Powell, & Sherwood, 2014).

At the beginning of the semester, I furnished each student with a blank composition book. I told students that they would be doing informal writing during each class period for which they would receive credit. In order to keep track of participation, I simply noted who was writing and whether anyone was not. However, noncompliance was not an issue with these students. (Other faculty using this strategy might opt to have students turn their journals in periodically for accountability purposes.)

I opened each class meeting with 7 to 10 minutes of informal journal writing in which students responded to a prompt about the topic for the day. For example, on a day that we were discussing the concept of the banality of evil, students were asked to respond to the following prompt: "How much of the evil in the world, along with our personal contributions, do you think is a product of a failure to *think*, of failing to have 'an internal dialogue' within ourselves about the moral and social consequences of our actions?" On another day, when we were exploring the idea of identifying and using one's personal strengths, the writing assignment opened with an anonymous quote: "Everybody is a genius. But if you judge a fish by its ability to climb a tree, it will live its whole life believing that it is stupid." Then came this prompt:

Spend a few moments thinking about this quote, and then write down your thoughts about it. You might think about answering some of these questions in your writing:

- Have you ever felt like "a fish trying to climb a tree"—in other words, like you were trying to do something that wasn't using your individual strengths and talents? If so, how did that feel?
- Think of several moments like that. What did they have in common?
- Can you think of one moment (or several) when you felt like you were doing what you were born to do because you were so good at it, or so happy, satisfied, or fulfilled doing it?
- Think of several moments like that. What did they have in common?
- When you think of what you love to do, what kind of themes emerge? For example, are you creating things? Are you building connections between people or ideas? Are you achieving a goal?

As shown in the "fish" prompt, I often provided several questions for reflection. I told students that they were welcome to respond to the original stimulus or one or several of the reflection questions. I did this to ensure students wrote the full time allotted and reflected thoroughly on the concepts before discussing them.

During this time, I played quiet instrumental music created specifically for reflection and study because this technique has been shown to improve or maintain positive affect during academic tasks (Dosseville, Laborde, & Scelles, 2012; Juslin, Liljeström, Västfjäll, Barradas, & Silva, 2008; Juslin & Västfjäll, 2008). In the second half of the course, I invited students to request specific music or bring in similar music that they wanted to share during our writing time. In addition, at the beginning and throughout the semester, I routinely told students to be ready to share their thoughts so that as they were writing, they were aware that they might be called on to explain what they had written about. Because both large- and small-group discussion offers learning benefits (Hamann, Pollock, & Wilson, 2012; Pollock, Hamann, & Wilson, 2011), I decided to alternate the starting formats from whole-group discussion to small-group before whole-group discussion to paired dialogue before whole-group discussion. This is the same pattern I used with the class the year before.

However, after adding the informal writing practice, the students were more likely to speak up and share their thoughts on the topics with the larger group. In fact, multiple students had their hands up waiting to speak. The year before there were often long minutes of silence after which I had to elaborate the verbal prompt in order to get a response.

I measured class participation informally by counting the number of students who shared a response with the entire class and the number of times during a class period when students did not spontaneously reply to a prompt. Compared with the first year I taught the course, I saw many more students communicating their opinions with the whole class and fewer instances of one or two talkative students dominating the discussion. I also noticed more instances of typically quiet students speaking up and disclosing their ideas and viewpoints. After implementing the informal writing exercise, I witnessed few, if any, times when no student responded to the verbal prompt.

I used informal notes to assess the effectiveness of the new strategy in not only broadening student participation but also advancing learning. After each class, I noted the quality of the discussion in response to two questions: Did the class as a whole engage in the discussion? Did the class as a whole appear to understand the concept being discussed and demonstrate this by participating actively in the discussion? This system gave me the chance to make quick notes as soon as class was over and the experience was still fresh. I then reviewed my notes as a whole at the end of the semester to see what patterns I found. The first pattern I identified was that overall the first-year students in the informal writing class participated more actively in whole-group discussion than the students in the previous nonwriting class. The second pattern that I saw was broader participation in whole-group discussion. In fact, very few, if any, students did not volunteer to share their thoughts with the class at least once. This practice appeared to increase both the number of students participating in class discussion and the quality of the discussion. The third pattern was that *all* the students actively wrestled with the complex issues under discussion, and this was evident from their contributions. I could determine which students grasped the issue (the majority) and which were struggling, and I could then give additional guidance to the latter group. Previously, I could not assess my students' understanding because too few of them spoke up. Thus, with greater quantity of participation came higher quality discussion.

The use of the informal writing practice in my first-year seminar worked so well that I implemented it in an upper-level undergraduate major course the next semester and achieved similar positive results. I highly recommend this strategy to instructors who want to lead discussions that include all students and explore the content in a deep, meaningful way.

To use informal writing most effectively, I offer the following pieces of advice. First, either provide students with a designated journal or have them bring a notebook or composition book that is dedicated to journaling alone. This helps students keep all of their journal entries together so that they can reflect on them in the middle and end of the term. Second, explain the value of the informal writing at the beginning of the term so they embrace the practice and do not mistake it for busywork. Third, use the strategy regularly and in the same way each time to ensure a consistent experience and practice. Otherwise students may fail to see its importance and its integral role in the coursework and class experience. Fourth, give students time to process what they have written even if you do not plan to have a whole-group discussion on the prompt. Just a paired dialogue or small-group exchange will allow them to express their own ideas, hear those of others, and talk through the issue.

The use of the contemplative pedagogy of informal writing has made my students active and thoughtful contributors to class discussions. It has opened the door for quieter students to let their voices be heard and given all students the time they need to form their thoughts before speaking. I intend to continue exploring this practice and its applications in the classroom.

References

Ambrose, S. A., Bridges, M. W., DiPietro, M., Lovett, M. C., & Norman, M. K. (2010). *How learning works: Seven research-based principles for smart teaching.* San Francisco, CA: Jossey-Bass.

Dosseville, F., Laborde, S., & Scelles, N. (2012). Music during lectures: Will students learn better? *Learning and Individual Differences, 22,* 258–262. doi:10.1016/j.lindif.2011.10.004

Ewell, W. H., & Rodgers, R. R. (2014). Enhancing student preparedness for class through course preparation assignments: Preliminary evidence from the classroom. *Journal of Political Science Education, 10*(2), 204–221.

Hamann, K. K., Pollock, P. H., & Wilson, B. M. (2012). Assessing student perceptions of the benefits of discussions in small-group, large-class, and online learning contexts. *College Teaching, 60*(2), 65–75. doi:10.1080/87567555.2011.633407

Hudd, S. S., Smart, R. A., & Delohery, A. W. (2011). "My understanding has grown, my perspective has switched": Linking informal writing to learning goals. *Teaching Sociology, 39*(2), 179–189.

Juslin, P. N., Liljeström, S., Västfjäll, D., Barradas, G., & Silva, A. (2008). An experience sampling study of emotional reactions to music: Listener, music, and situation. *Emotion, 8*(5), 668–683. doi:10.1037/a0013505

Juslin, P. N., & Västfjäll, D. (2008). Emotional responses to music: The need to consider underlying mechanisms. *Behavioral and Brain Sciences, 31*(5), 559–621. doi:10.1017/S0140525X08005293

Linton, D. L., Pangle, W. M., Wyatt, K. H., Powell, K. N., & Sherwood, R. E. (2014). Identifying key features of effective active learning: The effects of writing and peer discussion. *CBE—Life Sciences Education, 13*(3), 469–477.

Petko, D. D., Egger, N. N., & Graber, M. M. (2014). Supporting learning with weblogs in science education: A comparison of blogging and hand-written reflective writing with and without prompts. *Themes in Science & Technology Education, 7*(1), 3–17.

Pollock, P. H., Hamann, K., & Wilson, B. K. (2011). Learning through discussions: Comparing the benefits of small-group and large-class settings. *Journal of Political Science Education, 7*(1), 48–65. doi:10.1080/15512169.2011.539913

10

AVOIDING CRICKETS BY CREATING AN ORCHESTRA OF STUDENTS

Billy Strean

A gaggle of geese, a murder of crows, an orchestra of crickets. The image of crickets evokes the lone audible signal on a still night. The loud, persistent, chirping song of male crickets actually represents their attempts to attract females. If student culture had evolved differently, perhaps we could rely on undergraduates' mating desires to evoke more than ample participation. Unfortunately, however, those in our courses often seem to resemble those cricket species that happen to be mute. How do we transform a collection of taciturn students into an interacting team of vocal contributors?

The Problem

In my earliest days of teaching undergraduate students as a graduate assistant, I observed what my doctoral supervisor called the *eyes down effect*, where students would become fascinated by the marks on their desks the moment a question or an opportunity to engage was put to them. As I was alternating between teaching and being a student, I could empathize with the many legitimate concerns that might squelch students from volunteering their ideas. As I progressed into becoming the primary instructor for courses, I became increasingly curious about what generated the silences and what stimulated lively classroom conversations.

One of my first insights was that the questions or prompts that many faculty relied on might be the source of students' hush. As I sat as a student in a graduate seminar, I noted that the professor would ask what could be called

107

monological questions, queries that had one and only one correct answer. I began to call this approach *fishing*. It seemed the instructor cast the question into the sea of students and hoped to reel in a correct response. None of the three likely responses was desirable: (a) a student offers an incorrect response, and the instructor says some version of "Well, no, that's not it" and continues fishing, leaving one student a little disheartened and embarrassed; (b) a student quickly offers a correct response, and we thankfully get to move on; or (c) the most common eventuality, where we wait out a prolonged silence in which perhaps some students who know the correct answer ponder whether they want to be seen in an unfavorable light for answering, other students aren't sure if they have it and don't want to take the risk, and some students don't know but are hoping someone does so we can move forward.

This situation was painted in cinematic history as Ferris Bueller's teacher inquired repeatedly, "Anyone? Anyone? Does *anyone* know what Vice President Bush called this in 1980? *Anyone?* Something-d-o-o economics. 'Voodoo' economics. Anyone? *Bueller?*" (Jacobson & Hughes, 1986). This is the culmination of 75 seconds, in which he asks for anyone to answer a question 15 times and does not get a single response. Yes, it is a Hollywood caricature, but it is a meme 30 years later because of its resonance with many of our shared classroom experiences.

If we ask questions that have no relevance to students and call for nothing greater than recall, or we don't allow students sufficient time to think before a response is desired, then we have been the source of our rooms being mum. Back then I recognized that the invitations for participation and engagement mattered. Yet, I was a fair distance from recognizing what I came to believe was the most important source of the speechlessness. Those moments of cavernous quiet struck me both pedagogically and personally as problematic. Discussions are good because they increase active learning. If they aren't happening, if students are not motivated to think, then the quality of the education drops. Those instances were also painful to me individually.

Eventually I realized that I am a microcosm of the core issue behind this cricket conundrum. In our hearts, we all deeply want to connect with other human beings. At a cellular level, we want to move toward others; if you put two pieces of human protoplasm on a slide, they will rally to unite. Yet, concomitantly, we harbor a profound fear of rejection. Consider that not long ago in human history, being pushed out of the herd portended almost certain death. I believe that fear also lives in our genes. I felt a yearning to connect with students and a wish for them to connect with each other while experiencing hints of terror when I felt my attempts failed.

Now, every time I invite students to participate, I keep in mind this internal tug-of-war that they must face when choosing if they will accept. The universal challenge is exacerbated by the individual negative experiences that students have before university. During the past 25-plus years, I have explored the practically universal histories that students bring to the class-room. I have asked many rooms of students (and teachers and faculty in workshops) if they can remember at least one time when they felt shamed, humiliated, put down, or made wrong in a classroom. It is exceedingly rare to find an individual who cannot. I acknowledge that each person likely has at least one good reason not to participate. Maybe many of the students in your class were the smart ones, and when they answered correctly, a peer teased them for being a smarty-pants or the teacher's pet. Or perhaps they ventured a response and were dismissed or faced failing in front of their friends. We need to respect what can lie behind their reticence and construct spaces that stimulate participation.

Solving With Humanity and Community

Perhaps because of my own longings, I have sought ways to create human connection and a learning community environment that fosters engaging discussions. Although many useful strategies, techniques, and incentive sys-tems are available to promote discussion, I have come to believe that the interpersonal foundation provides the crucial basis for lively classroom con-versations. Some of the most cited works in higher education (e.g., Chick-ering & Gamson, 1987; Lowman, 1995) have asserted that a fundamental principle of effective teaching is increasing teacher-student contact and con-nection. Yet our classrooms can do more to meet students' needs for affilia-tion and promote engaging discussions.

I design the first day of every course with explicit attention to these issues. I begin by greeting each student with a handshake and an introduc-tion: "Hi, I'm Billy, what's your name?" As I meet the students, I ask them if they have met one or two of the students around them and introduce those who have not met before. They also complete an information sheet where they share their motivations, concerns, and (optionally) something interest-ing or goofy about themselves. We have a conversation during this first ses-sion about their mixed histories as learners, and I suggest ground rules as one way to counter their reservations about participation. Typical guidelines are "Be kind," which is a good catchall; "No killer statements (or gestures)," which helps us let down our armor; "Confidentiality," which is more essen-tial in some courses; and "Focus on the speaker," which discourages side conversations during class discussions.

More recently, both students and I have talked about the use of phones and texting. Students tell me about the volume of texting they see in other classes, but my classes have virtually no such problem, I believe, because of their high level of active engagement. I have witnessed and heard about some rather draconian approaches to trying to reduce this off-task behavior. But I see this potential challenge as a way to create an atmosphere of respect and dignity. Students and I can all agree that phones can be misused, and students admit to each other that they find it distracting. Instead of abolishing phone use completely, I tell students (just as I do other adults in workshops that I lead) that I recognize that they have lives, including something more important than this class at times. If a family health emergency or something urgent is looming, I ask that they keep their phone on vibrate and handle a call or text with the least possible disruption to class. My policy tends to produce a state of pleasant shock in the room and helps create an atmosphere that encourages the kinds of interaction that we all long for.

The first day can make a huge difference toward establishing the mood and openness of the class. In recent years I have been fortunate to teach classes of 24 to 36, and I have found that learning all of the students' names on the first day builds connections like magic. (When I have taught larger classes, I have taken photos of groups of students holding name cards and memorized as many names as I could.) My effort to learn names, admittedly easier for me than many, pays more than worthwhile dividends in facilitating discussions.

I also strive to be very aware of the fragility of the classroom dynamics. One bad moment can detonate all of the achievement of building community. So as a person who may enjoy sarcasm in other situations, I am vigilant about checking it at the door of the classroom. Even when a class may want me to put a student in his place with a sarcastic barb, I believe that my doing so will make students feel that I just drew blood from one of their own, and they may be next. Similarly, I must be the shaman (Campbell, 2008) who maintains the space and keeps us to our agreements of how we will treat each other. Through deliberate activities in which students get to know each other and conduct serious work in a space of lightheartedness, such regulating is rarely necessary.

Discussions, Dialogues, or Conversations?

With the interpersonal space developed and upheld, we have the environment to cultivate discussions and avoid that dreaded silence. Although we use the term *discussion* generically, as when we call some courses seminars and others lecture-discussions, we should consider, at least for our internal understandings, what discussion suggests. It comes from the same roots as *concussion* and *percussion* and can imply to hit with, smash apart, or talk over (picture a bad day in the House of Commons). Perhaps this term does not evoke such conflict for you. Other times, when I hear about *debates*, I sense they have their place, but I attach greater value to more appreciative interchanges in a world with too much adversarial communication. *Dialogues*, although often mistakenly believed to denote talking between two people, can involve more participants and refer to a "flow of meaning." I deliberately use the term *conversation* because it implies we are going to change together. Reflect for a moment, if you will, about a class where the instructor already knows the right answer and is seeing what the students can produce versus a situation in which we are all participating with curiosity and exploring how we may all shift through our engagement.

Does Everyone Want to Talk?

Faculty often teach to their own preferences, frequently unconsciously. For example, being an extrovert, I love group work and talking in class. In my early days of teaching, I didn't understand students who didn't talk in class. From their written work, I knew they were smart and wondered what it would take to get them to engage. I've become progressively more appreciative of individual differences and the plight of an introvert in highly social educational settings. Consequently, I have adapted a strategy (based on my experience with the late critical thinking expert Richard Paul) that gives everyone a few moments to write down his or her ideas in response to a question or prompt. After reminding the class that some people prefer to think on their own and others prefer to talk out their thoughts, I invite students to let others know when they want to start talking by standing up and pairing with the next person to stand up. (The mechanics of this may have to be altered to accommodate seating arrangements and physical ability.) Given the opportunity, some students will pop up within seconds while others will spend the entire time writing. Depending on the complexity of the topic or my desire to move to a full-class discussion, I might direct students to form groups of three or four. In addition to respecting individual differences, this approach primes the pump for the larger group discussion, probably because students have a chance to share and rehearse their ideas first.

Discussion Success?

Although it delights me when students participate actively in class, how do I know if a discussion effectively fulfills its intended learning outcomes?

I have voluminous anecdotal data that suggest students demonstrate deeper understanding of and a greater ability to apply concepts on papers and exams after discussions. But beyond these casual data, I also have used many classroom assessment techniques to ascertain what makes discussions more and less effective, and how particular discussions have served or not served students—for example, basic techniques like the one-minute paper or a four-square that asks (a) What worked well? (b) What didn't work? (c) What suggestions do you have? (d) What questions remain? My subjective sense has proven incomplete and negatively biased unless I felt like the energy was flowing and everything was clicking. Students' perceptions and comments have usually been more affirming and invaluable in making adjustments, such as honing the wording of my questions to sharpen clarity.

The Payoff: An Orchestra

I have borrowed a question from a colleague to show the value of talking: Which way do you think you would learn more: (a) preparing and delivering a lecture or (b) sitting and listening to a lecture? Of course, everyone says the former. Then, we might ask, why do we set up our courses so that the professor does the most learning? Classroom discussions, among other methods, lead us away from this perverse irony and transform passive listeners into active learners. The value of discussion shines through a wily remark from another colleague to a room of students enthusiastically engaged in group conversations: "Please stop learning. I want to talk more now." If we fail to establish the interpersonal dynamics that will facilitate students' lively engagement and participation, we doom ourselves to doing too much talking and depriving our students of rich opportunities to enhance their learning.

What could be more fulfilling than those moments when students are champing at the bit to add their ideas and the room is buzzing with energy and laughter? The efforts to create a learning community where such an occasion becomes a regular element of the course make it more than worthwhile. As students become willing contributors, nurturing their effective listening in discussions naturally follows. The singing species of crickets have good hearing, and learning how to listen appreciatively and supportively furthers the development of a high-functioning orchestra of students. The beauty of students' voices compared to the silence that crushes your soul and makes your stomach clench is inspiration to begin with the humanity of teaching and create communities that sing with conversation.

References

Campbell, J. (2008). *The hero with a thousand faces* (3rd ed.). Novato, CA: New World Library.

Chickering, A. W., & Gamson, Z. F. (1987). Seven principles for good practice in undergraduate education. *AAHE Bulletin*, 3–7.

Jacobson, J. (Producer) & Hughes, J. (Director and producer). (1986). *Ferris Bueller's day off* [DVD]. United States: Paramount Pictures.

Lowman, J. (1995). *Mastering the techniques of teaching* (2nd ed.). San Francisco, CA: Jossey-Bass.

SPICING UP STUDENTS' EDUCATION

The Use of Course-Based Undergraduate Research to Foster Student Communication

Heather Townsend

The Challenge: Bringing Relevancy and Cognitive Skills Into the Lab

True learning is more than memorization. Knowing the correct terminology for a concept or phenomenon is not the same as being able to speak meaningfully about it. Students often arrive on the first day of science class ready to memorize a significant amount of information but with no expectation to go any further. Given this mind-set, engaging them in meaningful and relevant discussion is challenging. Students come woefully unprepared to think deeply about the material or to communicate with each other about it. They sit quietly and write down what they are told but stare blankly when you try to induce them to discuss the material. They may memorize facts and figures, but unless they are convinced that those facts have real-world relevance to their lives and future careers, they quickly forget the content once the exams are over.

At my community college, the introductory microbiology course is intended for students interested in the nursing program and allied health fields, such as respiratory therapy and dental hygiene. The weekly three-hour lecture portion of the course focuses on microorganisms and their role in causing disease and is accompanied by a required weekly three-hour laboratory portion in which student groups conduct standard labs that typically result in the same outcomes that we aim for in the related lectures. These labs focus on handling specimens and cultures properly, identifying unknown bacteria in a sample, and identifying the presence of microorganisms in food and water.

Although these labs connected skills with the content, my students failed to see the labs' relevance to their future careers. After dutifully completing a lab, they walked away without discussing their experiences or reflecting on their processes. Further, the lab experience did not foster the creative thinking, problem-solving, or collaborative skills that the health professions require. Health practitioners must be able to think creatively and evaluate solutions beyond their textbooks because every situation can be drastically different and potentially life threatening. They also must be able to work as part of a team: Their success relies on listening to others and communicating clearly.

I wanted my students to understand the material, not just memorize it. I wanted them to experience genuine lab research, not just plod through what they perceived to be near pointless exercises. I wanted them to learn how to think and talk about the material effectively. So I had to change my labs. If I wanted my students to engage in discussion, I had to give them something worth discussing. I decided to implement a course-based undergraduate research experience (CURE) to foster deep learning and active discussion.

A Solution: The High-Impact Practice of Undergraduate Research

High-impact practices (HIPs) refer to several pedagogical strategies that strongly enhance student engagement, result in higher grades, foster peer discussion outside of class, enrich learning, and increase student exposure to diversity (Kuh, 2008). They also enhance overall satisfaction with the educational experience (Brownell & Swaner, 2009). Student involvement in undergraduate research is a proven HIP with tremendous educational benefits (Brownell et al., 2015; Corwin Auchincloss et al., 2014; Corwin, Graham, & Dolan, 2015; Hanauer & Dolan, 2014; Shortlidge, Bangera, & Brownell, 2016), especially improvements in students' communication and collaborative skills because they have to share and present their results (Swanson, Park Sarge, Rodrigo-Peiris, Xiang, & Cassone, 2016). Research embedded into a course (CURE) reaches many more students than a select stellar few.

Pragmatic challenges came with incorporating a CURE into a tight 15-week semester schedule. I had to keep all of the course content and skills practice, yet furnish the time for students to complete an entire research project. A summer institute at the University of Texas geared toward implementing CUREs helped me solve the logistics. In the end, I decided on a project that involved culturing 6 different species of bacteria and testing the effectiveness of various dilutions of household spices in inhibiting bacterial growth. Spices have been shown to have phenomenal antibacterial properties; this topic connected well with my goals for the course. The project was reasonable in scale, inexpensive, and relevant to the students given that bacterial resistance to chemicals mirrors antibiotic resistance. More importantly, I believed that the project would engage students in discussing how to overcome the challenges that research brings.

I designed the 13 weekly labs so that in each lab students would complete one small task, either in lab or during their study hours, to prepare them for the next step of the process. They had to keep lab notebooks so that I could check on their progress and completion of the prelab tasks. The student groups had to pick one spice for their research, test its effectiveness on the 6 species of assigned bacteria, and compare their results to those of other groups. My hope for this comparison process was to generate class discussion. At the end of the semester, the groups evaluated the effectiveness of their spice in restricting the growth of bacteria and presented their findings to the college community via a poster session. This session required students to discuss their projects not only with fellow biology students but also the larger academic community.

I feared that students would complain about the additional work and that some might drop the course. When I told them about the research requirement, their faces said it all: shock, fear, and dissatisfaction. Most did not understand what scientific research entailed, and for many, the word *research* apparently meant "write a 20-page term paper." To calm their fears, I explained that research is a calculated process and that I would guide them every step of the way. In addition, they would master the course material more deeply and, more importantly, learn key lessons about being a scientist or a healthcare provider. The project would engage them in ways that they didn't expect and stimulate discussion around their shared fears. Many remained dubious, which made me question whether a CURE offered *the* cure for getting disengaged undergraduates to meaningfully discuss concepts in microbiology.

My Observational Assessment

My fears were unfounded. The conversation that ensued was deafening! Without my prompting, without a list of premeditated questions, without a grade requirement, students began discussing the project. They eagerly engaged in conversation not only with members of their research group but also all the groups, and at times even with me. They problem-solved through unexpected situations and had animated discussions about the results they expected. This new classroom endeavor made them all equally vulnerable to the point that they felt comfortable enough to exchange ideas and suggestions with each other.

The class quickly surpassed my most optimistic expectations. Students came to lab better prepared and received better grades than students in previous semesters of the same course. Most importantly, they started to do the one thing they dreaded most: They started to talk.

I designed the assignments to promote discussion during the labs. At one point, students had to develop a chemistry equation for diluting the spices, and they came up with four different equations. They had to decide as a class which formula was both correct and practical in the limited time that we had for each lab. Merely asking for a mathematical formula sparked collaboration and serious discussion that led students to learn the required chemistry for the project.

At another point in the course, students had to pick the spice their group would be testing. I instructed each group to find scientific primary journals on two spices that they thought would inhibit bacterial growth. Several groups had selected and researched the same spices. I expected this and hoped it would create some discussion. But I didn't expect the passion that students felt about their preferred spice. Groups began to debate over who should have the privilege of using a given spice, supporting their claims with the primary literature that they found. I had never witnessed that level of discussion in a lab before and recognized that students' understanding of the material increased as a result of this discussion.

The research project created another group dynamic I hadn't seen before. Students felt more comfortable talking with each other because they were experiencing this challenge together. They often left their own lab tables to travel across the room to another lab group to discuss what they were doing. If a problem arose, I urged them to converse with one another to devise a solution.

On the day that students arrived to observe their experimental results, I could feel the electricity pulsing from their nerves as they walked through the lab doors. One of the students said that they woke up that morning feeling "like it was Christmas" and couldn't wait to get to lab to see their results. I had never heard of an entire class genuinely wanting to come to lab before!

I had expected that the various spices in different concentrations would yield different results. I even prepared the students for the possibility that they might not obtain the results that they expected. One of the groups had absolutely no results, meaning that the spice had no effect on any of the bacteria growing on the plate at any of the dilutions. The group was devastated, and the students blamed themselves (as a group) for doing something wrong to cause this "failure." I assured them that no effect simply meant that their spice was not effective, but this was still a result! I reminded them that in the real world not all antibiotics are effective against all bacteria. These negative results provoked a class-wide discussion on why this happened. The students deeply reflected on the chemistry involved as they developed many plausible explanations. One student even conducted a side study to test a secondary hypothesis about whether heating the spices to a certain temperature would change their effectiveness (it did!). This collective analysis of the variety of results and explanations never would have occurred during the cookie-cutter labs of the past; they had engendered no passion and no discussion.

This level of engagement increased discussion not only during lab but also lectures. Although the lectures replicated those of previous semesters, these students engaged with them differently. Hands went up. They asked questions to be sure they understood a concept as well as they had to before lab day arrived. They also made insightful comments as they linked ideas from lecture to experiences in lab.

The Students' Assessment

To evaluate students' perception of the new CURE, I used a survey with two open-ended questions:

1. In what ways did you personally benefit from doing the research project in this class?
2. In what ways do you feel more or less prepared for the workforce after doing the research project?

I assured students that their responses would be confidential and I would not see their feedback until after the semester had ended.

All students stated that, despite being nervous initially, they saw great value in the research experience. Many reported that the CURE required them to practice better time-management skills (something I had never intended to address). They recognized the benefit of participating in a class-wide project rather than more isolated, lecture-based laboratory activities. They said that they greatly enjoyed the interaction, collaboration, and discussion and spoke positively about preparing and sharing their research through a poster presentation, which they felt helped them develop important presentation skills. Most importantly, they all felt better prepared for the workforce with stronger communication skills.

Give Them Something to Talk About

The main lesson that I learned through this class experience is simple: If you want your students to engage in discussion, make sure to give them something they think is worth discussing. For microbiology, a CURE was an excellent solution. It provided students with hands-on, real-life experience; developed their problem-solving skills; gave them practice at true collaborative work; and spurred serious discussion.

Class-wide research may not be a solution for all academic fields. Yet many courses in the biological, physical, and social sciences and possibly languages and history can accommodate it. CUREs entail a good deal of work in the beginning, but the payoff in student engagement and discussion is well worth it. You can find many resources (e.g., websites, books, conferences, colleagues) to help you initiate a CURE for your students. Support sites such as CUREnet, ccuri.org, and cur.org offer many opportunities to collaborate and create a CURE. A research project will get students organized and keep them talking, both in and out of the classroom. Not only will they learn research they will also experience deep engagement.

Some advice: Try to have the course planned week by week and determine exact dates on which certain assignments will be given, worked on, and due. Have students do a written or oral reflection each week to promote expression of thoughts and ideas. These reflection pieces will help students engage in the types of deep thinking that really spur discussion. Preparing their thoughts will also help them to have something worth saying in class. In my course, we regularly discussed what had happened in the previous week's lab, what to expect that day in lab, and what we anticipated in the next week's lab. This required my students to think and communicate about the course material multiple times. The implementation of a CURE into my course has changed my pedagogical outlook for the better.

References

Brownell, S. E., Hekmat-Scafe, D. S., Singla, V., Chandler Seawell, P., Conklin Imam, J. F., Eddy, S. L., . . . Cyert, M. S. (2015). A high-enrollment course-based undergraduate research experience improves student conceptions of scientific thinking and ability to interpret data. *CBE–Life Sciences Education, 14*(2), 1–14.

Brownell, S. E., & Swaner, L. E. (2009). High-impact practices: Applying the learning outcomes literature to the development of successful campus programs. *Peer Review, 11*(2), 26–30.

Corwin, L. A., Graham, M. J., & Dolan, E. L. (2015). Modeling course-based undergraduate research experiences: An agenda for future research and evaluation. *CBE–Life Sciences Education, 14*, 1–13.

Corwin Auchincloss, L., Laursen, S. L., Branchaw, J. L., Eagan, K., Graham, M., Hanauer, D., . . . Dolan, E. L. (2014). Assessment of course-based undergraduate research experiences: A meeting report. *CBE–Life Sciences Education, 13*, 29–40.

Hanauer, D. I., & Dolan, E. L. (2014). The project ownership survey: Measuring differences in scientific inquiry experiences. *CBE–Life Sciences Education, 13*, 149–158.

Kuh, G. D. (2008). *High-impact educational practices: What they are, who has access to them, and why they matter.* Washington, DC: Association of American Colleges & Universities.

Shortlidge, E. E., Bangera, G., & Brownell, S. E. (2016). Faculty perspectives on developing and teaching course-based undergraduate research experiences. *BioScience, 66*, 54–62.

Swanson, H. I., Park Sarge, O., Rodrigo-Peiris, T., Xiang, L., & Cassone, V. M. (2016). Development of a course-based undergraduate research experience to introduce drug-receptor concepts. *Journal of Medical Education and Curricular Development, 3*, 57–66.

APPLYING STUDENTS' INSIGHTS FOR ENGAGING INQUIRY IN A BLENDED COURSE

Janelle DeCarrico Voegele

The Challenge

It was getting late, and I was still in class: Postsecondary Curriculum, a graduate course taken by about 25 master's degree students in the Educational Leadership and Policy Program. In the online classroom, where the boundaries of space and time spill over into the rest of life, I took a moment to look out my window and sigh before heading into the last student discussion thread I'd yet to join. In this blended course, I saw my students in both the on-campus and the online classrooms, but the online discussions didn't match the classroom discussions for energy or participation. Posts were missing or seemed perfunctory, and responses were lackluster. I was tempted to dive through the computer screen and exhort students to please, *please* engage more fully with their whole selves online, as they did on campus. Or rather, as they usually did on campus, except when it came to applying insights from online discussions to their project work. In those moments, some students participated, but not all; some seemed challenged to remember what had occurred online. I had yet to cross the web discussion barrier.

This chapter describes my inquiry into students' blended learning experiences with discussion: I explored the literature on students' interactions in blended formats; I analyzed students' feedback across multiple blended courses on my campus; and, finally, I engaged in a coinquiry with my students as I applied what I learned from the literature and feedback to this blended course. I synthesized what I learned with the learner-centered principles proposed by Cullen, Harris, and Hill (2012) to develop the sustained, deeper level discussion and learning I was after in my blended course.

The Inquiry

I first turned to the research literature to learn more about the nature of student engagement in blended courses. Some evidence suggests that blended courses have impacted instructors' pedagogical approaches to inquiry, increasing their confidence in a facilitative role (e.g., Kaleta, Skibba, & Joosten, 2007). However, many faculty assume that online discussions in blended courses are less problematic than those in fully online courses because in the former students have a chance to meet one another in class. This assumption, I soon learned, is not supported (Starenko, Vignare, & Humbert, 2007). For example, although some research documents students' positive perceptions of increased interaction with peers online (Jackson & Helms, 2008), other studies reveal students' preferences for additional face-to-face discussion available in classrooms (Mitchell & Forer, 2010) and challenges in developing a sense of community (e.g., So & Brush, 2008).

While I conducted my literature review, I was also involved in a blended learning initiative on my campus that allowed me to conduct student learning assessments in other blended courses. This project evolved into a research study with student feedback from more than 50 undergraduate and graduate blended courses, yielding data that uncovered three themes or factors associated with students' favorable perceptions of course interactions: (a) preparation for collaborative activities, (b) active instructor engagement both online and face-to-face, and (c) the purposeful integration of online and classroom activities to deepen inquiry (Voegele, 2014).

How would I apply what I had learned to discussions in my own courses? The answers were not straightforward. For example, both the blended learning literature and student feedback on my campus had underscored the importance of instructors' active participation online and in the classroom, but I also knew from experience (and from other instructors on my campus) how time intensive such practices could be in blended course discussions. More importantly, better discussions weren't always the result of more participation. I needed more than discrete strategies for actively facilitating distance and classroom discussions; I also needed to revisit the fundamental purposes of such practices in my blended course. The following learner-centered framework supplied the crucial second piece to my blended course revision.

Back to Class: Rethinking Discussion in a Learner-Centered Framework

The primary learning objectives of Postsecondary Curriculum are for students to apply insights from postsecondary curriculum theory to develop or redesign a curriculum intervention for adult learners and to implement most of these interventions in their postsecondary settings. Because students have a great deal of autonomy over and enthusiasm for their projects, I had been baffled in the past by lackluster online discussions, as well as a disconnect between the project ideas discussed online and in class.

Therefore, I decided to reframe the role of discussions by applying the learner-centered framework described by Cullen and colleagues (2012). This framework is based in four principles of course design: richness, recursion, relations, and rigor. *Richness* refers to "examining layers of meanings and interpretations of experience" via activities "rich in dialogue among participants" (Cullen et al., 2012, p. 47). It implies that dialogue not only addresses the course content but also enriches and shapes the course, as students construct coherence across diverse perspectives. *Recursion* refers to "a nonlinear approach . . . whereby students reflect on their learning over time, examining how their understandings change" (p. 51). Such an approach means relinquishing some content and focusing on fewer ideas more deeply. *Relations* emphasizes the relationships among all aspects of the course in a creative social activity involving reflective discussion. Learning involves considerable attention to "the individual's seeing things from multiple perspectives and understanding the effect of different contexts" (p. 52). *Rigor* refers to "elements that provide opportunities for integrative learning—that is, learning that is organized around problems or issues rather than strictly discipline content" (p. 57).

I wanted students to experience, rather than just read about, learner-centered teaching, and for some time I had approached this course with learner-centered principles in mind. However, I was humbled by what I may have assumed about the role of discussions in fostering a learner-centered environment. Was the course truly rich in dialogue among participants, or were students talking past one another about concepts in their hurry to get to the next checklist item? Were discussions activities during which students had ample time to explore their own and others' frames of reference, or did it feel more like a Twitter feed to get in as much information as possible through separate portions of classroom and online time? Did students experience discussions as interrelated with other parts of the course or distinct from the "real business" of getting their projects done? In other words, how could the role and function of discussion itself become more learner centered?

The Application of Both the Study Result Themes and Learner-Centered Principles

To begin reassessing the role of discussion in my course, I listed the three themes related to positive student perceptions of course interactions from my campus-wide study of blended courses, my previous course design related to each theme, and my revised design for discussion inspired by learner-centered principles. These three components are found in Table 12.1.

Preparation for Collaborative Activities: Codesigning Discussion

Drawing on my study's finding about the importance of deliberate preparation for online and classroom discussions, I redesigned the online discussions in collaboration with the students. I insisted only that discussions would be expected both online and in class, and that students would split into groups that alternated speaking and active listening roles to encourage more dialogue online (explained in the following).

On the first day of the course, I invited students to propose the goals for the discussions in the context of course outcomes and other course activities. They proposed the following, beginning with the most important:

- Get to know peers; develop community.
- Share and get others' perspectives on course ideas.
- Support each other on the development of field projects.

To this list, I added:

- Create continuity between online and face-to-face classrooms.

Having agreed on the major goals for discussions, we moved to students' ideas for the role of discussion in the course. For online discussions, students wanted to focus on challenges and successes related to their field projects. They preferred this idea over responding to instructor-developed questions over course concepts, as during the previous course offerings. However, I wanted students to discuss course concepts to ensure they would prepare for class and to enable me to assess their understanding, as I had before.

To serve both my students' and my own preferences, I drew on my findings about relevance and integration as well as the principles of recursion and rigor in encouraging students to pose research questions related to their projects. For example, a student working in the student affairs field on new student orientation asked how the event could better prepare first-generation college students for their first quarter. These types of student-generated

TABLE 12.1
Previous and Revised Discussion Framework,
Based on Blended Discussion Themes

Blended Study Theme	Previous Course Design	Revised Course Design	Learner-Centered Principles
Preparation for collaborative activities online	Instructor gave students guidelines and prompts to discuss course readings online. Online discussions were less engaging than campus class discussions.	Students and instructor create part of the online discussion activity together. What would they consider engaging and relevant?	Relations: Curriculum creation is reimagined as a social activity connected to other aspects of the course.
Instructor engagement in both course formats	Instructor demonstrated engagement online by commenting and responding to discussion threads over course material and facilitating discussion in class. Student response to instructors' online engagement in discussion was infrequent.	Demonstrate engagement online: Instructor is coach and guide to students who take turns as "responders," whose role it is to encourage dialogue. Demonstrate engagement in class: Instructor makes explicit the ways that online inquiry connects to and shapes campus class inquiry.	Richness: Dialogue shapes curriculum and fosters coherence across diverse frames of reference.
Integration of classroom and distance discussion activities	Instructor used discussion prompts to encourage application of online course discussion over material to classroom discussion of projects. It was difficult to move discussion beyond a surface level.	Display online discussion threads at the beginning of campus class; students highlight themes that are then applied to project issues and challenges. Resulting insights are then used to plan for upcoming online discussion.	Recursion: Students reflect on how their understandings change over time. Rigor: Opportunities are provided for integration focused on real issues and problems.

questions prompted rich, sustained discussions over time. To further encourage richness in the dialogue across projects, I also proposed that students offer ways that current course concepts might resolve the issues and problems they identified. They agreed, as long as their initial online discussions of course concepts could be exploratory, which would allow for freer interaction and exchange of ideas online. I then proposed how I would assist in integrating online and classroom discussions.

Integrating Classroom and Distance Inquiry

I proposed to the class that I would join the online discussions in a listening role, functioning as a consultant when needed. I would be happy to contribute feedback when requested, but I wanted primarily to focus on how our in-person class time could facilitate deeper inquiry across primary ideas and questions that arose during online interactions. At first some students were confused and wondered if I was saying that I wouldn't be participating online. I responded that I definitely would be, as I hoped would be evident in the ways that our campus time together reflected their online work. We decided to revisit this plan after two or three discussion cycles.

Active Engagement in Both Formats

I wasn't surprised by students' confusion about my active listening role online. In my study, I had learned that students in blended courses found it disheartening when their instructors seemed disconnected from the online discussions. However, seeing learning as a social activity in part constructed by participants (Cullen et al., 2012), I wanted to distribute the online listening role across the class, to underscore our shared responsibility for tracking the class's understandings and insights as they changed over time. As mentioned previously, I had already included in the online discussion assignment the roles of speakers and responders. I proposed that when speakers (half of the class) posted, they would remind us of the research question connected to their project, discuss the project and their progress, and then explore the issues they raised related to course concepts. Responders (other half of the class) would try to resolve the project issues raised by speakers, offering their own perspectives and frames of reference. The roles would reverse for each discussion cycle. I intended to join the responders when needed, clarifying areas of confusion and proposing how we might further explore and resolve those during our classroom time. I hoped that this would reduce their burden of replying to large numbers of posts but still demonstrate my presence to encourage dialogue.

Blended Discussions

Although campus classes followed various formats, the following is a typical example of how classroom discussions flowed from previous interaction online and prepared for upcoming online inquiry: I opened campus class sessions by displaying the previous week's online discussion threads on a large screen at the front of the room. Next, the students reflected on these threads with activities such as think/pair/share or drawing graphic representations of the online discussions. This activity immediately involved everyone so that no student could passively watch and "coast" on others' initial connections. Then, I used questions to help students reflect on and integrate their graphic representations and further analyze those ideas in relation to relevant curricular frameworks. Often these questions were inspired by ideas from the online discussions, which I acknowledged, and I could see the students engage when their discussion insights were extended in class. I also hoped this would reinforce my active involvement both in class and online.

Students then developed themes across their individual insights and/or graphic representations of online discussions. For example, they grouped the previously mentioned research question about the preparation of first-generation students with other questions related to curriculum and equity for underrepresented college students. Students connected this theme to course material on praxis approaches to curriculum development and, in small groups, proposed how they would specifically use insights from integrative discussions in their project drafts. Because the online discussions had often begun with unresolved project issues, this format brought the online and campus discussions full circle in a more rigorous and recursive way.

Finally, the class conducted a meta-analysis of the previous week's inquiry cycle: What was effective? What could be changed? To further integrate the two class formats and better prepare students for the upcoming inquiry cycle, I asked the students to propose how they could extend their classroom insights into the upcoming online activities. They alternated the role of "scribe" and wrote the ideas on the course website to ensure that we would remember them at the next online session.

Outcomes

I assessed the effectiveness of my new approaches to online and classroom discussions on three criteria: student engagement, perceptions of integration, and student learning.

Student Engagement

The class was much more engaged in online discussion. Because discussions now began with real problems and issues related to projects, they were infused with a passion and curiosity that fueled more lively and insightful exploratory connections with course material. The number of replies and threads often exceeded the minimum expectations, and the online discussions came closer to the dialogue that often occurred during the campus classes. Course assessments showed that students strongly agreed that I was present online, even though I now shared the responder role with the class and saved a great deal of time.

During classroom sessions, building and reflecting on previous online discussions reinforced the role of both course formats. As we reconstructed the themes from online discussions, I incorporated them into classroom activities and discussion. Students were invested in extending and integrating the themes that they had helped to identify, and I felt my role shift continually from expert to coach as students increasingly came to see the larger social, cultural, and political implications of curriculum change from multiple perspectives.

Perceptions of Integration

When asked about the discussions in both course formats, students were much more likely to describe them as connected. Because the inquiry cycle now began with their own curriculum projects, they made increasingly substantive contributions to class discussion over time. Concomitantly, my role shifted to that of weaver or storyteller, helping students create shared meaning across their diverse backgrounds, curriculum perspectives, and experiences.

Student Learning

Overall, the students' work demonstrated deeper learning, as evidenced by their insightful integration of course concepts and application to the field projects. Students also monitored their own progress. Their final self-reflections contained many specific examples from both online discussions and in-class peer activities.

Lessons Learned

From this case I learned (or was reminded of) the following lessons about discussions in blended courses:

- *Showcasing relevance in and connections among curriculum, course structure, and discussions.* The improved discussions were partially due to their grounding in relevant connections among the course content, the students' prior experience, their curriculum work, their personal and professional interests, and the ways that connecting all of these helped students learn from how their own understandings changed over time.
- *Making explicit the role of discussion in both course formats.* It helped that the online and classroom discussions could build together toward a common goal.
- *Revisiting the goals for discussion with the class.* I learned that my goals for discussion and those of my students were not always the same, but the result of our dialogue was a new shared purpose for discussion that may not have occurred otherwise.

Conclusion: The Cycle Continues

Dialogue among participants is central to a rich and relevant curriculum (Cullen et al., 2012). In this blended course, we began with a class discussion on discussions, which resulted in inquiry as part of a cycle that integrated face-to-face and classroom formats. By beginning inquiry with discussions situated in real and relevant curriculum experiences, the class was better prepared to move through the recursive cycles of sustained and integrative critical reflection needed for their professional development as educational leaders. Blended courses are well suited to cycles of individual and shared construction of meaning. In the end, discussions in both formats were more effective to develop a course community, its themes repeatedly woven throughout the tapestry of the course.

References

Cullen, R., Harris, M., & Hill, R. R. (2012). *The learner-centered curriculum: Design and implementation.* San Francisco, CA: Wiley.

Jackson, M. J., & Helms, M. M. (2008). Student perceptions of hybrid courses: Measuring and interpreting quality. *Journal of Education for Business, 84,* 7–12.

Kaleta, R., Skibba, K., & Joosten, T. (2007). Discovering, designing and delivering hybrid courses. In A. G. Picciano & C. D. Dziuban (Eds.), *Blended learning: Research perspectives* (pp. 111–143). Needham, MA: Sloan Consortium.

Mitchell, P., & Forer, P. (2010). Blended learning: Perceptions of first-year geography students. *Journal of Geography in Higher Education, 34*(1), 77–89.

So, H. J., & Brush, T. A. (2008). The content analysis of social presence and collaborative learning behaviors in a computer-mediated learning environment. In C. K.

Looi, D. Jonassen, & M. Ikeda (Eds.), *The 13th Annual Conference on Computers in Education* (pp. 413–419). Amsterdam, NE: IOS Press.

Starenko, M., Vignare, K., & Humbert, J. (2007). Enhancing student interaction and sustaining faculty instructional innovations through blended learning. In A. G. Picciano & C. D. Dziuban (Eds.), *Blended learning: Research perspectives* (pp. 161–178). Needham, MA: Sloan Consortium.

Voegele, J. D. (2014). Student perspectives on blended learning through the lens of social, teaching and cognitive presence. In A. G. Picciano, C. D. Dziuban, & C. R. Graham (Eds.), *Blended learning: Research perspectives* (Vol. 2, pp. 93–103). New York, NY: Routledge.

SOLVE SEVERAL ONLINE COURSE CHALLENGES WITH STUDENT CRITIQUES OF PRIMARY LITERATURE

David M. Wilson

Challenge 1: Isolated Students

Getting students to participate in discussions in an online chemistry course presents a number of opportunities and challenges for me. Chemistry can be challenging in a face-to-face environment, but it's even more so online. My institution, Parkland College, is a community college, and my course, Chemistry for Health Professions II, is offered only online. Many of the students do not live close to campus and never meet me or their classmates. Consequently, online students usually feel disconnected and isolated, which may contribute to high attrition rates (Angelino, Williams, & Natvig, 2007; Wei, Chen, & Kinshuk, 2012). Discussion forums can help alleviate these feelings by fostering interactions and a sense of social presence in online students (Gunawardena & Zittle, 1997), but only if students perceive them as authentic and truly interesting.

In the past, my students displayed little depth of thought in online forums and rarely went beyond the bare minimum required. I had to provide explicit details about the minimum number of posts and replies, the exact content expected, the number of words in a post or reply, and other mundane details. When I required reply posts, the situation was even worse; students rarely contributed more than a few encouraging words to their peers. In short, they seemed to view most online discussions simply as a task to check off their list. This likely did nothing to reduce the isolation and disconnectedness they experienced.

On positive side, most of the students in my class are working toward a bachelor of science in nursing (BSN) and already have some sort of certification or degree in the health professions, so they are fairly experienced, self-motivated students.

Challenge 2: Desired Science Outcomes

Virtually every science instructor I have spoken with acknowledges critical thinking as an important intended outcome of a science course, and I suspect the same is true in many other disciplines. Yet to the casual observer, most instructors do not appear to target critical thinking beyond providing students with a variety of contrived and narrowly focused problems. Instructors do not even agree on what *critical thinking* is. The definition I prefer comes from Lewis Vaughn (2008) in *The Power of Critical Thinking*: "The systematic evaluation or formulation of beliefs, or statements, by rational standards" (p. 4).

Another broad outcome that many science instructors would support is the ability to articulate the nature of science (NOS). My department engages in academic assessment every semester, and that process has identified shortcomings in students' understanding of NOS. Most science textbooks emphasize the findings of science rather than its process, which probably contributes to these shortcomings. Some authors attempt to rectify this (Freeman, 2016), but most media outlets basically ignore NOS.

In this case study, I describe an assignment I recently developed that engages students, generates longer posts without specifying word counts, yields more thoughtful replies to other students' posts, fosters critical thinking, instills a sense of NOS, and even gets rave reviews from my students. The assignment I describe in this case study requires critical thinking. It asks students to assess their beliefs about the effectiveness of certain medical therapies, evaluate the statements made by researchers of these therapies, formulate new beliefs or find support for existing beliefs based on primary evidence, and develop new statements that reflect their beliefs in view of this new evidence. No other assignment I have given in my almost 25 years of college teaching experience has prompted more unsolicited, positive comments from my students, despite the fact that it is likely the most challenging assignment I have made.

The Assignment

In order to develop an authentic assignment that addressed the many challenges just described, I chose the topic of complementary and alternative medicines (CAMs). The topic encompasses a vast array of nontraditional medical applications such as acupuncture, yoga, aromatherapy, Reiki, and homeopathy. It works well for many reasons in the setting of a science course for the health professions. Patients often ask health professionals about CAMs, yet my students, most of whom already have a two-year degree or certificate and professional experience, have little to no knowledge of CAMs or their scientific standing.

The assignment uses the integrated discussion tool in our learning management system. I set up separate required discussions for each of 13 modules over a 16-week semester. The first 3 forums set the stage for the more challenging topics to come later. The first discussion asks students to research and discuss primary and secondary literature. In the second discussion, they select a journal article and post it to the forum. In some semesters, I ask students to pick articles on a common topic (often acupuncture), and in others I ask students to choose articles on any CAM field in which they are interested. Each approach has advantages and opportunities. In the third discussion, I ask students to research independently the topic of CAMs. I supply them with specific questions to address in their posts and encourage them to extend their responses to any related topic of interest.

With the groundwork laid, students critique various aspects of their articles in the next nine modules. The critiques target the journal, the authors, and the various sections of the articles. The thirteenth module asks students to reflect on how their perspective on CAMs or the medical field has changed and how they now perceive the vast primary literature on CAMs. Following are sample prompts for each of the discussion topics. (The complete prompts are more extensive than these samples.)

1. "Primary Literature": What are the characteristics of primary literature articles? What is their purpose? How would you go about finding an article in the primary literature?
2. "Article Selection": Please post information in this order: The medical issue being treated in each article, a link to the article, and the article citation.
3. "What is a CAM?": What is a CAM? How do CAMs differ from traditional medicine? Why is there a separate area of medicine devoted just to CAMs?
4. "Journals": Why are there separate journals for CAM research and traditional medical research? Who owns and operates the CAM journals? What vested interests, if any, do these journals have? Does the journal that published your chosen article have an adequate review process (e.g., peer review)?

5. "Authors": What are your authors' names and what are their credentials (degrees, certifications, licenses, etc.)? Who funds their research? What is their public persona in the social media sphere?

6. "Introduction": If the authors stated their main hypothesis, what is it? Do the authors discuss the background research that others have done related to the current study? Are there citations in the Introduction section?

7. "Methods I": Why are large sample sizes important in scientific studies? What process did the authors use to select their experimental subjects? Did your authors randomize the subjects?

8. "Methods II": What controls were used by the authors? Did the authors control for the placebo effect? If not, do you think they should have? Explain the importance of single-blind, double-blind, and other study methodologies used by the authors. If these were not used, explain why you think this is.

9. "Results I": Did the authors use graphs or tables? Why do you think they used these modes of communication? Did their graphs or tables include any statistical measurements (e.g., averages, standard errors, standard deviations, etc.)? Why do you think they chose (or chose not) to use these measures?

10. "Results II": [Students receive a resource explaining different types of validity.] What variables or phenomena are the authors trying to connect (e.g., yoga and cancer-induced pain)? Do the variables or phenomena have a logical connection? That is, is it reasonable to assume that one could in some way impact the other? Mention the specific type of validity you are addressing and explain why you think the authors did or did not provide valid results.

11. "Conclusions": Are the authors' conclusions consistent with the data? Do they leave out any conclusions that you think the data justify? Do they connect their own data with previously published results from similar studies?

12. "References": What types of journals do the authors cite in their bibliography? Are they CAM-type journals or more mainstream medical journals? How important do you think it is for the authors to have their work cited by others?

13. "Concluding Thoughts": What, if anything, has changed in your thinking about CAMs since the beginning of the semester? How will you respond to your patients who ask for a professional opinion about using CAMs in their own health care?

Evaluation of the Assignment: Methods

To assess the impact of this assignment on student isolation, I looked for evidence that students replied to one another with comments that showed respect, interest, and sincere inquiry. I used the length of replies to indicate interest and engagement with their classmates. I also carefully read their final module posts in which they reflected on the entire project.

To evaluate the impact of the assignment on critical thinking skills, I looked for evidence that the assignment affected the students' opinions on the validity of CAMs and, more generally, the primary literature. For example, I sought out comments suggesting that students recognized that not all primary literature is equally valid, that certain experimental methods are stronger than others, and that their beliefs about the efficacy of specific CAM therapies were in flux.

To examine the effect of the assignment on students' understanding of NOS, I looked for evidence that students were evaluating articles as objectively as possible and applying NOS concepts. Specifically, I considered their comments on sample sizes, the presence of appropriate controls, the use of double-blind methods, and so on. This effort reflected one of my reasons for developing this assignment in the first place, which was to help students see that not all primary literature is equally valid or strong. Traditional medical journals publish strong scientific findings, whereas most specialized CAM journals publish weaker findings.

I loosely monitored other metrics indicating that the forums were accomplishing other broad goals such as longer posts, more numerous posts beyond minimum requirements, depth of thought, and insightfulness.

Finally, I set up a reflections forum at the end of the semester to measure any changes in how the students perceived CAMs and the primary literature and to obtain their general assessment of the assignment.

Evaluation of the Assignment: Results

As the tone and thoughtfulness of their posts and replies suggested, students were engaged with each other. They were always extremely respectful of one another, although I would have liked to see them challenge each other a little more on the merits of their articles. As indicated in the final reflective posts, they clearly enjoyed learning about each other's topics and interacting virtually on a subject of common interest. The overall tone of the discussions and the unsolicited comments I received from students showed that they felt connected to their classmates through this common interest.

One of my favorite aspects of this assignment was the focus on critical thinking. Prompts for each discussion directed the students to focus on certain aspects in each section of the article and then to assess how well the authors had met the basic requirements of conducting and reporting primary research. Students found this assignment one of the most challenging and enjoyable they have ever had in a class.

As to whether students properly evaluated the validity and strength of their articles, their posts suggested there was room for improvement. Many people, including health professions students, have strong biases in favor of CAMs and the tendency to give authors the benefit of the doubt. Some students recognized weaknesses in an article's methods, but I suspect that these students came into the course with doubts about certain CAM claims. Probably a few of my students had much previous exposure to primary literature, so they couldn't fairly compare. One semester I asked students to pick two articles, one from a traditional medical journal and the other from a CAM article. Despite some logistical challenges, I will try this again in the future.

In the reflections forum, I saw evidence that students did recognize weaknesses in the CAM articles, but most of their responses were somewhat general. For example, some noted the possibility of bias by the journal and/or the authors, but only occasionally did they mention specifics such as the inadequate sample size, the lack of needed controls, and other research deficiencies. On a positive note, several students volunteered that they now felt more empowered to tackle other primary literature articles and knew what attributes to look for as evidence of quality.

I also noticed improvements in my students' understanding of NOS. In the CAM forums, students frequently commented about hypothesis-driven methodologies, the importance of checking for validity, the inadequate sample sizes, the absence of single-blind or double-blind methods, and other features that fall within NOS. However, most of these remarks represented responses to my specific prompts. Although a good start, this awareness may not constitute a cohesive set of beliefs or transfer to other situations. My department's academic assessment data may soon provide some insight on the transfer issue.

Unlike many online discussion assignments, this one was quite easy to grade. The number of words each student posted in each module ranged from about 200 to 400 for their original posts. With replies, the word count for a single module in a class of 20 easily exceeded 10,000. Therefore, I rarely critiqued the posts, and the replies somewhat alleviated this need. Most of my grading involved checking for minimum posting requirements and making sure that the posts were on topic and offered meaningful content, which characterized almost all the original posts. Replies, however, were sometimes lacking. Some students simply commented, "Good post," "I agree," or "Interesting perspective" without any substance that might extend the conversation. However, about half the class posted extensive replies that asked probing questions and made connections to their own articles or experiences.

The overall results of this assignment have encouraged me to continue to refine it over the years and given me confidence that my students are benefiting from my revisions. Most important, students have overwhelmingly reported that they enjoyed and benefited from this project. They have expressed how practical this assignment was in advancing their career development because most of them have fielded patient questions about various CAM therapies. In addition, I have seen far more volume posted for this assignment than any other discussion forum I created previously, and that volume has been neither trivial nor repetitive. Finally, the posts have provided a great deal of evidence that my students have strengthened their critical thinking skills.

Opportunities to Improve the Assignment

I see several ways of improving this assignment in the future. First, I plan to administer a pretest and posttest to assess my students' knowledge. The results will help me tweak the assignment to improve their learning.

Second, a few students have advised me to connect this assignment more explicitly to the course content—for example, to ask students to posit what physiological or biochemical mechanisms might be involved in these therapies. This kind of topic could generate interesting discussions and enhance the students' critical thinking skills.

Third, I am also considering initiating small-group discussions in which each group conducts a different critical review. The class could then complete this phase in less time, and the extra time could go to additional conversations on how CAMs might operate physiologically or biochemically. I could still require students to post replies to other groups to broaden their topical knowledge and interact with more of their peers.

As I mentioned previously, the quality of reply posts proved to be one of the weaknesses of this assignment, no doubt because students have less knowledge to draw on in formulating their replies. Small-group discussions where several students are working together on the same CAM topic, or even the same article, might help fill in holes in their knowledge.

Another possible shortcoming was the absence of my perspective on the topics. I pretty much stayed out of the exchanges. Perhaps I missed opportunities to correct student misconceptions or to call attention to relevant ideas that did not surface during the discussions. However, I did not want to inhibit the students' free exchange of ideas by challenging their posts.

Strategies for Adapting This Approach to Other Disciplines

Probably the single most important factor that makes this assignment work is that students see direct relevance to their careers, and virtually all of them plan to enter or advance in the health professions. But this assignment should be easily adaptable to many disciplines because almost any course content, even that of a general education course, can relate to various occupations, hobbies, or cultural themes. You might explore possible topics with your colleagues and gather data from assessment results, personal observations, and other sources to find out what topics in your discipline give your students the most trouble and pose challenges that they may face someday in their careers, civic lives, or personal lives. Structure your assignment around these topics to make it meaningful to your students.

You can manage your personal time by realizing that it is not necessary to read or comment on all the posts for students to benefit. While scanning them, jot down a few ideas you would like to share with the class. A single class reply at the end of a discussion can be very effective while saving you time and effort. You can tell students that your quizzes and exams will contain questions from the posts to encourage them to read more carefully.

References

Angelino, L. M., Williams, F. K., & Natvig, D. (2007). Strategies to engage online students and reduce attrition rates. *Journal of Educators Online, 4*(2), 1–14.

Freeman, S. (2016). *Biological science* (6th ed.). Boston, MA: Pearson.

Gunawardena, C. N., & Zittle, F. J. (1997). Social presence as a predictor of satisfaction within a computer-mediated conferencing environment. *American Journal of Distance Education, 11*(3), 8–26.

Vaughn, L. (2008). *The power of critical thinking: Effective reasoning about ordinary and extraordinary claims* (2nd ed.). New York, NY: Oxford University Press.

Wei, C., Chen, N. & Kinshuk. (2012). A model for social presence in online classrooms. *Education Technology Research and Development, 60*(3), 529–545. doi:10.1007/s11423-012-9234-9

FACULTY DISCUSSION GROUP RESOURCES

Jennifer H. Herman and Linda B. Nilson

This chapter presents writing prompts, discussion questions, and workshop ideas that educational developers and reading group leaders can use to engage faculty and graduate students with this book. We recommend that individual faculty begin with the reflective writing prompts. They should then dialogue with a partner around the prompts or the discussion questions and, to explore the ideas more fully, use the jigsaw framework or a similar learning community model.

For educational developers or those charged with the professional development of their peers or graduate students, we suggest using the workshop ideas for activities and private consultations and the discussion questions to launch small-group exchanges. Ideally, learning community members can read excerpts from the book and come prepared to discuss the accompanying questions. For graduate courses or teaching assistant development programs, this book can serve as a text and the resources as homework or in-class activities.

Writing Prompts

In addition to the uses previously mentioned, the following prompts can facilitate a peer-to-peer mentoring or a support model in which faculty who are interested in these topics have in-person, mutually supportive conversations:

- Reflect on when you usually use discussion in your teaching. What purpose do you intend for it to serve? What tends to work well?

- Think about times in which you've experienced challenges with discussion. What patterns do you see? Which do you think are related to the content? Your specific teaching style or approach? The discipline?
- To what degree have you shared your challenges with colleagues? If you have, what experiences have they shared? Have they offered any helpful suggestions?
- Some students present challenges: those who dominate, those who don't contribute, narcissists, inattentive students, those who launch personal attacks, and other types listed in chapter 2. Write or share one or more stories about your most challenging students; these may be specific stories or stories about the challenging types you see most frequently.
- What types of strategies have you used to help all students participate? What has worked well, and what hasn't? Why?
- How do you design discussion to meet learning objectives? What elements of chapter 3 do you incorporate into your course design or lesson planning?
- How do you assess either student learning or participation in discussion?
- Overall, what would you like to improve about discussions in your classes?

Discussion Questions

In this section, we offer discussion questions for chapters 1 through 5 and each of the case studies and then pose questions to help connect the chapters and the case studies. These questions can facilitate large- or small-group discussions and stimulate individual reflection.

Chapter 1

1. This chapter begins by distinguishing recitation and discussion. How does the distinction apply within the context of your discipline and your specific courses?
2. How do recitation and discussion differ in terms of how you involve students? How you facilitate the class? Where can you find appropriate recitation questions for your content?
3. What types of learning can discussion foster that recitation cannot? What do you think it means for discussion to be "leading students on a cognitive trip" (p. 3)?

4. Given the learning benefits that can accrue from discussion, which are the most relevant for your discipline? What are the limitations of discussion in your discipline?

5. This chapter explains that "the learning benefits of discussion accrue only when instructors know how to plan and lead one effectively" (p. 4) and offers four case studies to illustrate discussions gone awry. Select one or more of these case studies, and explain the factors that you think influenced the direction of the discussion. What happened and why? What could the instructor have done differently?

6. After the case studies, the chapter describes possible negative impacts of failed discussion on students and faculty. Which effects reflect your experience? What other negative repercussions can you add to this list?

Chapter 2

1. Chapter 2 addresses the first of 3 concerns in discussion: problematic student engagement. Which of the 12 principles to guide class discussion resonate with you, and why?

2. What are 3 concrete strategies derived from the 12 principles that you might try implementing in your classes?

3. Preparation is vital for discussion, yet research tells us that relatively few students do the assigned reading unless they are held accountable. Describe your experience in preparing students for discussion. How have you tried to hold them accountable for their preparation? What has worked, and what hasn't?

4. Have you used any of the discussion formats described in Principle 4 and Principle 5? If so, what was your experience? What might you try in a future class?

5. According to Principle 7, structures give students time to think before responding and lead to better discussion. Which strategies might work well in your classes?

Chapter 3

1. Chapter 3 describes 12 common discussion pitfalls, including 10 challenging student types and behaviors. Which are the most common challenges you've experienced in your classes?

2. What strategies have you tried to address challenging student types? What has worked well, and what hasn't? What insights or ideas from this chapter may help you mitigate these challenges in the future?

3. Chapter 3 closes with some strategies for synchronous and asynchronous online discussion. If you have taught online, what has been your experience with discussion? What has helped, and what hasn't? What strategies would you consider implementing in the future?

Chapter 4

1. Chapter 4 opens with three scenarios illustrating how discussion can disconnect from learning: superficial or off-topic comments, siloed remarks that don't build on previous contribution, and unsupported or biased opinions. Which of these have you heard (or read) in your classes? What was the impact on student learning?
2. Have you tried to incorporate others' successful discussion methods into your classes? To what extent have they transferred well into your context?
3. What previous experience have you had with backward design? Have you ever used it in course design?
4. Chapter 4 emphasizes the importance of understanding and articulating the function of the discussion within the larger course design. Although many faculty may have a sense of a discussion's purpose, far fewer articulate it and tie it to course objectives. What purposes does discussion serve in your courses? If you haven't written learning objectives for discussion before, try writing them now for one of your courses.
5. Do you ever use discussion to help students prepare for an assessment, to assess the learning itself, or both? If you do, how do you help students see the connection between the discussion and graded assignments or exams? How well does the discussion actually help prepare them for these assessments? How do you know?
6. Do you share your grading rubrics with students? How can you tie these to a discussion to help increase student engagement and learning?
7. How can discussion serve as each piece in the content-experience-reflection framework? What role does it usually serve in your courses?
8. Chapter 4 ends by analyzing what went wrong in the three scenarios and suggesting changes to strengthen the connection between discussion and learning. How would you have advised the instructor in each of these scenarios based on the principles in this chapter?

Chapter 5

1. Chapter 5 recommends ways to assess discussion. Have you assessed discussion in your classes? If so, how?

2. One approach focuses on assessing the class's participation and engagement as a whole. Drawing on the suggested ideas, how might you implement this in your classes?

3. How do you assess whether a discussion has helped students meet the course learning objectives? What strategies from the text resonated with you?

4. Many instructors want to assess individual students' contributions, particularly for participation grades. How have you assessed this?

5. Have you ever tried anything like the participation rubric, participation log, or participation portfolio described in this chapter? How well might any of these approaches work in your context?

6. Why is it important to assess discussion at all in your courses? What are the benefits for doing so and the possible ramifications for not doing so?

Chapter 6 (Festle Case)

1. In her case, Festle describes challenges in getting students to move beyond "fact-based recitation" (p. 71), particularly in disciplines that they may erroneously view as being only about memorization. Have you faced this in your classes? How does Festle overcome this obstacle?

2. She is also challenged by polarized, exaggerated debates that "result in much heat but little light" (p. 72). Have you had discussions in your classes that you'd describe this way? How do they evolve, and how can you frame or structure discussion to avoid this situation?

3. Festle applies *deliberative dialogue* to address her challenges. How would you describe this strategy? What are its implications for civic engagement and discourse?

4. How does Festle create structures to ensure that students prepare for and contribute to discussion?

Chapter 7 (Marquart and Drury Case)

1. Marquart and Drury tackle the challenge of converting a traditionally face-to-face class into a synchronous online format. They start the course with concerns about maintaining high levels of engagement because online learners are easily distracted. Have you taught or participated in a live, online discussion? If so, what are other challenges? What are benefits? What surprised you in this case?

2. To reduce potential anxiety, the authors let their students chat via text rather than appear on webcam while supporting those who chose to

venture out of their comfort zones. How do you think their approach impacted students?

3. Marquart and Drury used a rubric to evaluate students on the quality of their contributions, yet some of them pushed back on this. What were their concerns? What other student concerns might arise when evaluating the quality of discussion in other contexts?

4. At the end of each class, the instructors elicited student feedback. What purpose did this feedback serve, and how does it tie into the design practices described in chapter 3?

Chapter 8 (Shapiro Case)

1. Shapiro takes on the challenge of getting a class of introverts to talk. How do you distinguish among introverts, disengaged students, and unprepared students?

2. Shapiro employs a method called *collaborative autoethnography*, which relies heavily on individual responsive writing. How does this technique resolve her challenge?

3. When Shapiro encountered crickets after asking students to report out, she shifted to which two structured approaches? How would you adapt these approaches to your context?

4. The author assesses discussion using student evaluations, journals, and final papers. What information about the effectiveness of a discussion does each indicator supply? Does your institution's student evaluation form have items related to student engagement in discussion? If not, can you add such an item on your own?

Chapter 9 (Shewmaker Case)

1. To increase engagement in discussion, Shewmaker focuses on connecting course content to students' interests and real-world applications. When have you done this in your courses, and what was the result?

2. What are the benefits of having students write informally before discussion, as Shewmaker does in her classes?

3. Increased participation allows her to use discussion to assess her students' understanding of course concepts. Have you assessed your students' understanding through discussion? How do you gauge whether silent students understand the concepts?

4. Shewmaker recommends giving students space to process in pairs or small groups as an intermediary step between informal writing and full-class discussion. How does this step benefit students or increase participation?

Chapter 10 (Strean Case)

1. Strean warns against *fishing*, a recitation-style approach in which you try to solicit a correct response. What are some problems with this approach? When might it be appropriate or effective in teaching?

2. According to Strean, students' fear of rejection, shame, or humiliation at being wrong discourages participation, and it stems from both survival instincts and past experiences. Can you share examples from your own experience, either as student or as instructor, that support or counter his contention?

3. This case describes several strategies to promote an "interpersonal foundation" (p. 109) for discussion. What exactly does Strean do, and what similar techniques have you used? Have you found that these activities make a difference?

4. After reviewing assessment data, Strean found that his subjective sense of the success of discussion was negatively biased. Have you ever collected data on your students' perceptions of a discussion? If so, did they confirm your expectations, or were you, like Strean, surprised by the results?

Chapter 11 (Townsend Case)

1. Before instituting discussion, Townsend gives several reasons why it might benefit her microbiology lab course. If you teach in a science, technology, math, or engineering (STEM) field, how can discussion promote learning in your courses?

2. Townsend's class discussions support a course-embedded research project. How can discussion complement larger research or project-based assignments in your courses?

3. How does Townsend's use of discussion to support a major assignment reflect the concepts addressed in chapter 3?

4. Townsend's approach enhances student enthusiasm and engagement. What about it do you think generates this reaction?

Chapter 12 (Voegele Case)

1. Voegele's introduction describes the online version of crickets: missing, perfunctory, or lackluster posts. Have you led or participated in asynchronous online discussions? If so, to what extent have you experienced what Voegele describes?

2. In her blended course, she observes a disconnect between the content discussed online and in person. What may be causing this lack of transference?

3. In the hope of making the class more learner centered, Voegele asks her students to propose goals for the discussions. Would it make sense for you to try this? What do you think your students would say?

4. Voegele adopts an active listening role in the online discussions. When facilitating online discussion, how active a role should instructors play? What are the benefits and drawbacks to commenting regularly versus listening actively and stepping in infrequently, if at all?

Chapter 13 (Wilson Case)

1. Wilson faced two challenges in his online chemistry course: minimalistic, isolated student posts and the need to foster critical thinking skills. What challenges in your courses might motivate you to rethink the role of discussion?

2. Wilson's 13 modules include sequenced questions scaffolding a larger assignment. What are the benefits of making discussion topics progressively more challenging? How might this work with your course content?

3. How does Wilson's assignment leverage external research to enhance learning through discussion? How does it develop critical thinking skills?

4. How does Wilson evaluate online discussion? What are other options?

Connecting the Cases With Chapters 2 Through 5

1. How does each case study apply or incorporate the 12 principles? What concrete strategies do the instructors use that reflect these principles? Which principles seem to get the most attention in each case study?

2. Chapter 3 describes common discussion challenges, including difficult student types. Which of these do you see at play in each of the case studies? What strategies do the instructors apply to prevent or remedy these challenges?

3. To what degree does each case study follow the design process described in chapter 4? Identify the learning objectives in each case. How does discussion connect with course assessment? What role does discussion play: content, experience, or reflection?

4. Chapter 5 lists three categories of assessment for discussion: student engagement in the discussion as a whole, student learning (i.e., achievement of the learning objectives) through the discussion, and the value of individual student contributions. How do the instructors in each case study assess the effectiveness of discussion? Which categories of assessment do they use? Which category best serves your purposes?

Workshop Ideas

Here are suggestions for workshops to aid instructors in encouraging discussion.

Strategy Demonstrations

This book describes a number of discussion strategies, such as the gallery walk and the fishbowl, that faculty and graduate students can best learn how to implement by experiencing firsthand. Either an educational developer or a peer can lead participants through one or more of these using almost any content. Because this is experiential learning, it is important to give participants time to reflect on the experience and discuss how and why they might use the strategy in their own classes.

Discussion Design Workshop

Many institutions offer course design workshops or institutes in which a facilitator guides participants through the backward design process. During the program, faculty design a course and receive helpful peer and facilitator feedback. This model adapts well to discussion design following the process outlined in chapter 4.

Jigsaw Book Club

In the jigsaw, described in chapter 2, each member of a small discussion group (typically three to five people) reads a different text and shares a summary and reflections during a discussion. Faculty groups can jigsaw the contributors' case studies with each member sharing a different case study and each case serving as a springboard for identifying themes and approaches.

Crowdsourcing Discussion

Crowdsourcing is a discussion-based, collaborative format that relies on group problem-solving. First, participants share, either electronically or in an initial face-to-face meeting, discussion challenges that they'd like the group to address collectively. Second, the group selects one challenge and talks through it, preferably in person, suggesting prevention measures and solutions. Alternatively, group members can ask questions of the person presenting the challenge or seek remedies in this book.

REFERENCES

Al-Shalchi, O. N. (2009). The effectiveness and development of online discussions. *Journal of Online Teaching and Learning, 5*(1), 104–108.

Ambrose, S. A., Bridges, M. W., DiPietro, M., Lovett, M. C., & Norman, M. K. (2010). *How learning works: 7 research-based principles for smart teaching.* San Francisco, CA: Wiley.

American Dialect Association. (2016). All of the words of the year, 1990 to present. Retrieved from https://www.americandialect.org/woty/all-of-the-words-of-the-year-1990-to-present#2016

Anderson, L. W., & Krathwohl, D. R. (Eds). (2001). *A taxonomy for learning, teaching, and assessing: A revision of Bloom's taxonomy of educational objectives.* New York, NY: Longman.

Andrews, T. M., Leonard, M. J., Colgrove, C. A., & Kalinowski, S. T. (2011). Active learning *not* associated with student learning in a random sample of college biology courses. *CBE Life Science Education, 10*(4), 394–405. doi:10.1187/cbe.11-07-0061

Angelo, T. A., & Cross, P. K. (1993). *Classroom assessment techniques: A handbook for college teachers.* San Francisco, CA: Jossey-Bass.

Archer, C. C., & Miller, M. K. (2011, April). Prioritizing active learning: An exploration of gateway courses in political science. *PS, Political Science and Politics,* 429–434.

Associated Press. (2017). *Associated Press Stylebook.* New York, NY: Author.

Augustine and Culture Seminar (ACS). (2008). *Learning communities rubric for evaluating class participation.* Villanova University, Liberal Arts and Sciences. Retrieved from http://www1.villanova.edu/villanova/artsci/acsp/resources/rubric.html

Bali, M., & Greenlaw, S. (2016, September 12). Tips for inclusive teaching. *The Chronicle of Higher Education.* Retrieved from http://www.chronicle.com/blogs/profhacker/tips-for-inclusive-teaching/62747

Bandura, A. (1986). *Social foundations of thought and action: A social cognitive theory.* Englewood Cliffs, NJ: Prentice Hall.

Barkley, E. F. (2010). *Student engagement techniques: A handbook for college faculty.* San Francisco, CA: Jossey-Bass.

Barkley, E. F., Major, C. H., & Cross, K. P. (2014). *Collaborative learning techniques: A handbook for college faculty* (2nd ed.). San Francisco, CA: Jossey-Bass.

Bartlett, T. (2017, February 17). The shaky science of microaggression. *The Chronicle of Higher Education.* Retrieved from http://www.chronicle.com/article/The-Shaky-Science-of/239150

Biggs, J., & Tang, C. (2011). *Teaching for quality learning* (4th ed.). Maidenhead, UK: Open University Press.

Bligh, D. A. (2000). *What's the use of lectures?* San Francisco, CA: Jossey-Bass.

Block, L. (2016, March 4). In favor of trigger warnings in college debate. *The Chronicle of Higher Education, 62*(25), B11–B13.

Bloom, B. S. (1956). *A taxonomy of educational objectives: The classification of educational goals. Handbook 1: Cognitive domain.* New York, NY: Longmans, Green & Co.

Bold, M. (2001). When a student feels stupid. *National Teaching and Learning Forum, 10*(2), 1–4.

Bonwell, C. C., & Eison, J. A. (1991). *Active learning: Creating excitement in the classroom* (ASHE-ERIC Higher Education Report No. 1). Washington, DC: George Washington University, School of Education and Human Development.

Bowen, J. A., & Watson, C. E. (2017). *Teaching naked techniques: A practical guide to designing better classes.* Hoboken, NJ: Wiley.

Bransford, J. D., Brown, A. L., & Cocking, R. R. (1999). *How people learn: Brain, mind, experience, and school.* Washington, DC: National Academies Press.

Bronte, C. (1847). *Jane Eyre.* London, UK: Smith, Elder & Co.

Brookfield, S. D., & Preskill, S. (2005). *Discussion as a way of teaching: Tools and techniques for democratic classrooms* (2nd ed.). San Francisco, CA: Jossey-Bass.

Brookfield, S. D., & Preskill, S. (2016). *The discussion book: 50 great ways to get people talking.* San Francisco, CA: Jossey-Bass.

Brooks, D. (2011, March 21). Getting students to talk. *The Chronicle of Higher Education.* Retrieved from http://www.chronicle.com/article/Getting-Students-to-Talk/126826

Burchfield, C. M., & Sappington, J. (2000). Compliance with required reading assignments. *Teaching of Psychology, 27*(1), 58–60.

Cardon, L. S. (2014). Diagnosing and treating Millennial student disillusionment. *Change: The Magazine of Higher Learning, 46*(6), 34–40.

Carroll, J. (2003, May 2). Dealing with nasty students: The sequel. *The Chronicle of Higher Education.* Retrieved from http://www.chronicle.com/article/Dealing-With-Nasty-Students-/18794

Cashin, W. E., & McKnight, P. C. (1986). *Improving discussion.* IDEA Paper #15. Center for Faculty Evaluation and Development, Kansas State University.

Center for Research on Learning and Teaching (CRLT). (n.d.) *Guidelines for discussing difficult or controversial topics.* Ann Arbor, MI: University of Michigan. Retrieved from http://www.crlt.umich.edu/publinks/generalguidelines

Chylinski, M. (2010). Cash for comment: Participation money as a measurement, reward, and formative feedback in active class participation. *Journal of Marketing Education, 32*(1), 25–38.

Clayson, D. E., & Haley, D. A. (2013). An introduction to multitasking and texting: Prevalence and impact on grades and GPA in marketing classes. *Journal of Marketing Education, 35,* 26–40. Retrieved from http://jmd.sagepub.com/content/35/1/26.full.pdf+html

Conderman, G. (2017). Question of the day promotes class participation. *Teaching Professor, 31*(3), 6. Retrieved from http://cdn.magnapubs.com/pdfs/TP1703.pdf

Corbett, B. A., Constantine, L. J., Hendren, R., Rocke, D., & Ozonoff, S. (2009). Examining executive functioning in children with autism spectrum disorder, attention deficit hyperactivity disorder and typical development. *Psychiatry Research, 166*, 210–222. Retrieved from http://dx.doi.org/10.1016/j.psychres.2008.02.005

Crenshaw, D. (2008). *The myth of multitasking: How "doing it all" gets nothing done.* San Francisco, CA: Jossey-Bass.

Cummings, C. A. (2015). Rethinking the fishbowl discussion strategy: A mechanism to construct meaning and foster critical thinking and communication skills through student dialogue. *Journal of Health Education Teaching Techniques, 2*(3), 23–37.

Dallimore, E. J., Hertenstein, J. H., & Platt, M. B. (2008). Using discussion pedagogy to enhance oral and written communication skills. *College Teaching, 56*(3), 163–170.

Dallimore, E. J., Hertenstein, J. H., & Platt, M. B. (2016). Creating a community of learning through classroom discussion: Student perceptions of the relationships among participation, learning, comfort and preparation. *Journal on Excellence in College Teaching, 27*(3), 137–171.

Delaney, E. (1991). Applying geography to the classroom through structured discussions. *Journal of Geography, 90*(3), 129–133.

DeSurra, C., & Church, K. A. (1994, November). *Unlocking the classroom closet: Privileging the marginalized voices of gay/lesbian college students.* Paper presented at the Annual Meeting of the Speech Communication Association, New Orleans, LA.

Docan-Morgan, T. (2015). The participation log: Assessing students' classroom participation. *Assessment Update, 27*(2), 6–7.

Doyle, T., & Zakrajsek, T. (2013). *The new science of learning: How to learn in harmony with your brain.* Sterling, VA: Stylus.

Duncan, D. K., Hoekstra, A. R., & Wilcox, B. R. (2012). Digital devices, distraction, and student performance: Does in-class cell phone use reduce learning? *Astronomy Education Review, 11.* Retrieved from http://www.colorado.edu/physics/EducationIssues/papers/Wilcox/Duncan_2012_AER.pdf

Dweck, C. S. (2016). *Mindset: The new psychology of success.* New York, NY: Ballantine Books.

Eberly Center for Teaching Excellence. (2008). *Solve a teaching problem: One student monopolizes class.* Retrieved from https://www.cmu.edu/teaching/solveproblem/strat-monopolizes/monopolizes-01.html

Eberly Center for Teaching Excellence. (n.d.). *Tools for assessment. Rubric for assessing student participation.* Retrieved from https://www.cmu.edu/teaching/assessment/examples/courselevel-bycollege/cfa/tools/participationrubric-cfa.pdf

Ewens, W. (2000). Teaching using discussion. In R. Neff & M. Weimer (Eds.), *Classroom communication: Collected readings for effective discussion and questioning* (pp. 21–26). Madison, WI: Atwood.

Fernandes, R. (2016, February 16). In a charged climate, colleges adopt bias response teams. *The Chronicle of Higher Education.* Retrieved from: http://www.chronicle.com/article/In-a-Charged-Climate-Colleges/235120

Fink, L. D. (2003). *Creating significant learning experiences: An integrated approach to designing college courses.* San Francisco, CA: Jossey-Bass.

Fink, L. D. (2013). *Creating significant learning experiences: An integrated approach to designing college courses* (2nd ed.). San Francisco, CA: Jossey-Bass.

Foerde, K., Knowlton, B. J., & Poldrack, R. A. (2006). Modulation of competing memory systems by distraction. *Proceedings of the National Academy of Sciences of the United States of America, 103*(31), 11778–11783. Retrieved from http://www.pnas.org/content/103/31/11778.full

Forster, F., Hounsell, D., & Thompson, S. (1995). *Tutoring and demonstrating: A handbook.* Edinburgh, UK: University of Edinburgh, Center for Teaching, Learning, and Assessment.

Francek, M. (2006). Promoting discussion in the science classroom using gallery walks. *Journal of College Science Teaching, 36*(1), 27–31.

Francek, M. (2016). *What is gallery walk?* Science Education Resource Center, Carleton College. Retrieved from: http://serc.carleton.edu/introgeo/gallerywalk/what.html

Freeman, S., Eddy, S. L., McDonough, M., Smith, M., Okoroafor, N., Jordt, H., & Wenderoth, M. P. (2014). Active learning increases student performance in science, engineering, and mathematics. *Proceedings of the National Academy of Sciences of the United States of America, 111*(23), 8410–8415. doi:10.1073/pnas.1319030111

Freire, P. (1970). *Pedagogy of the oppressed* (M. Bergman Ramos, Trans.). New York, NY: Herder and Herder.

Gayle, B. M., Cortez, D., & Preiss, R. W. (2013). Safe spaces, difficult dialogues, and critical thinking. *International Journal for the Scholarship of Teaching and Learning, 7*(2), article 5. Retrieved from http://digitalcommons.georgiasouthern.edu/ij-sotl/vol7/iss2/5/

Gelbar, N. W., Smith, I., & Reichow, B. (2014). Systematic review of articles describing experience and supports of individuals with autism enrolled in college and university programs. *Journal of Autism Developmental Disorders, 44,* 2593–2601. doi:10.1007/s10803-014-2135-5

Georgic, J. (2015). *Neurotransmitters and learning.* Retrieved from https://www.hastac.org/blogs/joegeorgic/2015/04/22/neurotransmitters-and-learning

Gilmore, T. N., & Schall, E. (1996). Staying alive to learning: Integrating enactments with case teaching to develop leaders. *Journal of Policy Analysis and Management, 15*(3), 444–457.

Gobbo, K., & Shmulsky, S. (2014). Faculty experience with college students with autism spectrum disorders: A qualitative study of challenges and solutions. *Focus on Autism and Other Developmental Disorders, 29*(1), 13–22. doi:10.1177/1088357613504989

Gooblar, D. (2015, March 18). Getting them to stop talking. *The Chronicle of Higher Education.* Retrieved from https://chroniclevitae.com/news/945-getting-them-to-stop-talking

Hadi, Z., & Sepler, A. (2016). *Forward space guidelines.* Ann Arbor, MI: Program on Intergroup Relations, University of Michigan.

Hall, R. (1982). *The classroom climate: A chilly one for women?* Washington, DC: Association of American Colleges & Universities.

Hanson, D. (2006). *Instructor's guide to process-oriented guided-inquiry learning.* Stony Brook, NY: Stony Brook University.

Herman, J. H., & Nilson, L. B. (2016, November). *A discussion on discussion on deep learning.* Roundtable at the annual conference of the Professional and Organization Development (POD) Network in Higher Education, Louisville, KY.

Hewitt, L. E. (2010). Individual differences in intervention response in children and adults with autism spectrum disorders. In A. L. Weiss (Ed.), *Perspectives on individual differences affecting therapeutic change in communication disorders* (pp. 131–149). New York, NY: Psychology Press.

Hoeft, M. E. (2012). Why university students don't read: What professors can do to increase compliance. *International Journal for the Scholarship of Teaching and Learning, 6*(2). Retrieved from http://academics.georgiasouthern.edu/ijsotl/v6n2.html

Hollander, J. A. (2002). Learning to discuss: Strategies for improving the quality of class discussion. *Teaching Sociology, 30*(3), 317–327.

Howard, J. R. (2015). *Discussion in the college classroom: Getting your students engaged and participating in person and online.* San Francisco, CA: Jossey-Bass.

Huang, S., Blacklock, P. J., & Capps, M. (2013, April 30). *Reading habits of college students in the United States.* Paper presented at the Annual Meeting of the American Educational Research Association, San Francisco, CA.

Hurtado, S., Milem, J., Clayton-Pedersen, A., & Allen, W. (1999). *Enacting diverse learning environments: Improving the climate for racial/ethnic diversity in higher education.* Washington, DC: The George Washington University.

Jaschik, S. (2016, August 29). The Chicago letter and its aftermath. *Inside Higher Education.* Retrieved from https://www.insidehighered.com/news/2016/08/29/u-chicago-letter-new-students-safe-spaces-sets-intense-debate

Johnstone, A. H., & Su, W. Y. (1994). Lectures—A learning experience? *Education in Chemistry, 35,* 76–79.

Junco, R. (2012a). In-class multitasking and academic performance. *Computers in Human Behavior, 28,* 2236–2243. Retrieved from http://www.sciencedirect.com/science/article/pii/S0747563212001926

Junco, R. (2012b). The relationship between frequency of Facebook use, participation in Facebook activities, and student engagement. *Computers & Education, 58*(1), 162–171. Retrieved from http://www.sciencedirect.com/science/article/pii/S0360131511001825

Junco, R. (2012c). Too much face and not enough books: The relationship between multiple indices of Facebook use and academic performance. *Computers in Human Behavior, 28,* 187–198. Retrieved from http://www.sciencedirect.com/science/article/pii/S0747563211001932

Junco, R., & Cotton, S. R. (2012). No A 4 U: The relationship between multitasking and academic performance. *Computers & Education, 59*(2), 505–514. Retrieved from http://www.sciencedirect.com/science/article/pii/S036013151100340X

Karp, D. A., & Yoels, W. C. (1976). The college classroom: Some observations on the meaning of student participation. *Sociology and Social Research, 60*(4), 421–439.

Kastens, K. (2010, November 29). Should we call on non-volunteering students? [Web log post]. Retrieved from https://serc.carleton.edu/earthandmind/posts/nonvolunteers.html

Kiewra, K. A. (1985). Providing the instructor's notes: An effective addition to student notetaking. *Educational Psychologist, 20*, 33–39.

Kiewra, K. A. (2005). *Learn how to study and SOAR to success.* Upper Saddle River, NJ: Pearson Prentice Hall.

Knowles, M. S. (1984). *The adult learner: A neglected species* (3rd ed.). Houston, TX: Gulf.

Kolb, D. A. (1984). *Experiential learning: Experience as the source of learning and development.* Englewood Cliffs, NJ: Prentice-Hall.

Kolodner, J. (2002). Facilitating the learning of design practices: Lessons learned from an inquiry into science education. *Journal of Industrial Teacher Education, 39*(3), 9–40.

Kosslyn, S. M. (1994). *Image and brain: The resolution of the imagery debate.* Cambridge, MA: MIT Press.

Kustra, E. D. H., & Potter, M. K. (2008). *Green guide: No 9. Leading effective discussions.* London, ON, Canada: Society for Teaching and Learning in Higher Education.

Kuznekoff, J. H., & Titsworth, S. (2013). The impact of mobile phone usage on student learning. *Communication Education, 62*(3), 233–252. Retrieved from http://www.tandfonline.com/doi/full/10.1080/03634523.2013.767917

Lahey, M., & Rosen, S. (2014). *Neurotransmitters and learning, memory and developmental disorders.* Retrieved from http://www.childrensdisabilities.info/allergies/developmentaldisorderslearningmemory2.htm

Lakey, G. (2010). *Facilitating group learning: Strategies for success with diverse adult learners.* San Francisco, CA: Jossey-Bass.

Larkin, J. H., & Simon, H. A. (1987). Why a diagram is (sometimes) worth ten thousand words. *Cognitive Science, 11*, 65–99.

Leamnson, R. (1999). *Thinking about teaching and learning: Developing habits of learning with first year college and university students.* Sterling, VA: Stylus.

Leamnson, R. (2000). Learning as biological brain change. *Change: The Magazine of Higher Learning, 32*(6), 34–40.

Lempert, D., Xavier, N., & DeSouza, B. (1995). *Escape from the ivory tower: Student adventures in democratic experiential education.* San Francisco, CA: Jossey-Bass.

Lepp, A., Barkley, J. E., & Karpinski, A. C. (2014). The relationship between cell phone use, academic performance, anxiety, and satisfaction with life in college students. *Computers in Human Behavior, 31,* 343–350. Retrieved from http://www.sciencedirect.com/science/article/pii/S0747563213003993#

Lewes, D., & Stiklus, B. (2007). *Portrait of a student as a young wolf: Motivating undergraduates* (3rd ed.). Pennsdale, PA: Folly Hill Press.

Lockhart, E. A. (2016). Why trigger warnings are beneficial, perhaps even necessary. *First Amendment Studies, 50*(2), 59–69.

Lukianoff, G., & Haidt, J. (2015, September). The coddling of the American mind. *Atlantic.* Washington, DC: Atlantic Media Company. Retrieved from https://www.theatlantic.com/magazine/archive/2015/09/the-coddling-of-the-american-mind/399356/

Maki, P. L. (2010). *Assessing for learning: Building a sustainable commitment across the institution.* Sterling, VA: Stylus.

Mayer, R. E. (2005). Introduction to multimedia learning. In R. E. Mayer (Ed.), *The Cambridge handbook of multimedia learning* (pp. 1–15). Cambridge, UK: Cambridge University Press.

Mayer, R. E. (2009). *Multimedia learning* (2nd ed.). New York, NY: Cambridge University Press.

Mayer, R. E., & Moreno, R. (2003). Nine ways to reduce cognitive load in multimedia learning. *Educational Psychologist, 38*(1), 43–52. Retrieved from http://www.uky.edu/~gmswan3/544/9_ways_to_reduce_CL.pdf

Mayer, R. E., & Sims, V. K. (1994). For whom is a picture worth ten thousand words? Extensions of a dual coding theory of multimedia learning. *Journal of Educational Psychology, 86*(3), 389–401.

Mazefsky, C. A., & White, S. W. (2014). Emotion regulation: Concepts and practice in autism spectrum disorder. *Child and Adolescent Psychiatric Clinics of North America, 23,* 15–24. doi:10.1016/j.chc.2013.07.002

Maznevski, M. L. (1996). *Grading class participation.* Center for Teaching Excellence, University of Virginia. Retrieved from http://cte.virginia.edu/resources/grading-class-participation-2/

McCoy, B. (2013). Digital distractions in the classroom: Student classroom use of digital devices for non-class related purposes. *Journal of Media Education, 4*(4), 5–14. Retrieved from http://en.calameo.com/read/000091789af53ca4e647f

McGonigal, K. (2005). Using class discussion to meet your teaching goals. *Speaking of Teaching, 15*(1), 1–6. Retrieved from http://web.stanford.edu/dept/CTL/Newsletter/discussion_leading.pdf

McGuire, S. Y. (2015). *Teach students how to learn: Strategies you can incorporate into any course to improve student metacognition, study skills, and motivation.* Sterling, VA: Stylus.

McIntosh, P. (1989). White privilege: Unpacking the invisible knapsack. *Peace and Freedom Magazine,* 10–12. Philadelphia, PA: Women's International League for Peace and Freedom.

McKeachie, W. J. (2002). *Teaching tips: Strategies, research, and theory for college and university teachers* (11th ed.). Boston, MA: Houghton Mifflin.

McKeachie, W. J., & Svinicki, M. (2014). *McKeachie's teaching tips: Strategies, research, and theory for college and university teachers* (14th ed.). Belmont, CA: Wadsworth, Cengage Learning.

Miller, M. D. (2014). *Minds online: Teaching effectively with technology.* Cambridge, MA: Harvard University Press.

Miller, R. L., & Benz, J. J. (2008). Techniques for encouraging peer collaboration: Online threaded discussion or fishbowl interaction. *Journal of Instructional Psychology, 35*(1), 87–93.

Millis, B. J., & Cottell, P. G., Jr. (1998). *Cooperative learning for higher education faculty.* Phoenix, AZ: American Council on Education and Oryx Press.

Moreno, R., & Mayer, R. E. (1999). Cognitive principles of multimedia learning: The role of modality and contiguity. *Journal of Educational Psychology, 91*(2), 358–368.

Nathan, R. (2005). *My freshman year: What a professor learned by becoming a student.* Ithaca, NY: Cornell University Press.

Nilson, L. B. (2016). *Teaching at its best: A research-based resource for college instructors* (4th ed.). San Francisco, CA: Jossey-Bass.

Nilson, L. B., & Weaver, B. E. (Eds.). (2005). *New directions for teaching and learning No. 101: Enhancing learning with laptops in the classroom.* San Francisco, CA: Jossey-Bass. Retrieved from http://onlinelibrary.wiley.com/doi/10.1002/tl.181/pdf

Ophir, E., Nass, C., & Wagner, A. D. (2009). Cognitive control in media multitaskers. *Proceedings of the National Academy of Sciences of the United States of America.* Retrieved from http://www.pnas.org/content/early/2009/08/21/0903620106.full.pdf+html

Oregon Health & Science University. (n.d.). *Examples of rubrics for assessing online forum posts.* Retrieved from http://www.ohsu.edu/xd/education/teaching-and-learning-center/academic-technology/upload/Assessing-Forums-with-Rubrics-Handout.pdf

Paivio, A. (1971). *Imagery and verbal processes.* New York, NY: Holt.

Paivio, A. (1990). *Mental representations: A dual coding approach.* New York, NY: Oxford University Press.

Paivio, A., & Csapo, K. (1973). Picture superiority in free recall: Imagery and dual coding? *Cognitive Psychology, 5,* 176–206.

Paivio, A., Walsh, M., & Bons, T. (1994). Concreteness effects on memory: When and why? *Journal of Experimental Psychology: Learning, Memory, and Cognition, 20*(5), 1196–1204.

Palloff, R. M., & Pratt, K. (2003). *The virtual student: A profile and guide to working with online learners.* San Francisco, CA: Jossey-Bass.

Pascarella, E., & Terenzini, P. (1991). *How college affects students: Findings and insights from twenty years of research.* San Francisco, CA: Jossey-Bass.

Pugliese, C. A., & White, S. W. (2014). Brief report: Problem solving therapy in college students with autism spectrum disorders: Feasibility and preliminary efficacy. *Journal of Autism Developmental Disorders, 44,* 719–729. doi:10.1007/s10803-013-1914-8

Quaye, S. (2012). Think before you teach: Preparing for dialogues about racial realities. *Journal of College Student Development, 53*(4), 542–562.

Retherford, K. S., & Schreiber, L. R. (2015). Camp Campus: College preparation for adolescents and young adults with high-functioning autism, Asperger Syndrome, and other social communication disorders. *Top Language Disorders, 35*(4), 362–385.

Robinson, B. D., & Schaible, R. (1993). Women and men teaching "Men, Women, and Work." *Teaching Sociology, 21,* 363–370.

Robinson, D. H., Katayama, A. D., DuBois, N. E., & Devaney, T. (1998). Interactive effects of graphic organizers and delayed review of concept application. *Journal of Experimental Education, 67*(1), 17–31.

Robinson, D. H., & Kiewra, K. A. (1995). Visual argument: Graphic organizers are superior to outlines in improving learning from text. *Journal of Educational Psychology, 87*(3), 455–467.

Robinson, D. H., & Molina, E. (2002). The relative involvement of visual and auditory working memory when studying adjunct displays. *Contemporary Educational Psychology, 27*(1), 118–131.

Robinson, D. H., & Schraw, G. (1994). Computational efficiency through visual argument: Do graphic organizers communicate relations in text too effectively? *Contemporary Educational Psychology, 19*, 399–414.

Robinson, D. H., & Skinner, C. H. (1996). Why graphic organizers facilitate search processes: Fewer words or computationally efficient indexing? *Contemporary Educational Psychology, 21*, 166–180.

Roehling, P. V., Vander Kooi, T. L., Dykema, S., Quisenberry, B., & Vandlen, C. (2011). Engaging the Millennial Generation in class discussions. *College Teaching, 57*, 1–6.

Rogers, S. L. (2013). Calling the question: Do college instructors actually grade participation? *College Teaching, 61*, 11–22.

Rosen, L. D., Carrier, L. M., & Cheever, N. A. (2013). Facebook and texting made me do it: Media-induced task-switching while studying. *Computers in Human Behavior, 29*, 948–958. Retrieved from http://dx.doi.org/10.1016/j.chb.2012.12.001

Ruan, J., & Griffith, P. L. (2011). Supporting teacher reflection through online discussion. *Knowledge Management and E-Learning: An International Journal, 3*(4), 548–561.

Shirts, G. (1977). *BáFá BáFá: A cross-culture simulation.* Del Mar, CA: Simulation Training System.

Skibba, K., Moore, D., & Herman, J. (2013). Pedagogical and technological considerations designing collaborative learning using educational technologies. In J. Keengwe (Ed.), *Research perspectives and best practices in educational technology integration* (pp. 1–27). Hershey, PA: IGI Global.

Smith, H. (2009). The foxfire approach to student and community interaction. In L. Shumow (Ed.), *Promising practices for family and community involvement during high school* (pp. 89–104). Charlotte, NC: Information Age Publishing.

SPRING. (2015). *Systems thinking and action for nutrition: A working paper.* Arlington, VA: USAID/Strengthening Partnerships, Results, and Innovations in Nutrition Globally (SPRING) Project.

Springer, L., Stanne, M. E., & Donovan, S. S. (1999). Effects of small-group learning on undergraduates in science, mathematics, engineering, and technology: A meta-analysis. *Review of Educational Research, 69*(1), 21–51.

Stanny, C. J. (2010). *Rubric for class participation.* Center for University Teaching, Learning, and Assessment, University of West Florida. Retrieved from http://uwf.edu/media/university-of-west-florida/offices/cutla/documents/Rubric-for-class-participation-stanny-(5).pdf

Stevens, D. D., & Levi A. J. (2012). *Introduction to rubrics: An assessment tool to save grading time, convey effective feedback, and promote student learning* (2nd ed.). Sterling, VA: Stylus.

Sue, D. W. (2010). *Microaggressions in everyday life: Race, gender, and sexual orientation.* Hoboken, NJ: Wiley.

Suskie, L. (2009). *Assessing student learning: A common sense guide* (2nd ed.). San Francisco, CA: Jossey-Bass.

Svinicki, M. (2004). *Learning and motivation in postsecondary classrooms.* San Francisco, CA: Jossey-Bass.

Talbert, R. (2017). *Flipped learning: A guide for higher education faculty.* Sterling, VA: Stylus.

Taylor, P. (2001). *Gallery walk.* Retrieved from http://www.cct.umb.edu/gallerywalk.html

Tigner, R. B. (1999). Putting memory research to good use: Hints from cognitive psychology. *College Teaching, 47*(4), 149–152.

Tindell, D. R., & Bohlander, R. W. (2012). The use and abuse of cell phones and text messaging in the classroom: A survey of college students. *College Teaching, 60*(1), 1–9. Retrieved from http://www.tandfonline.com/doi/full/10.1080/87567555.2011.604802

Tulving, E. (1985). How many memory systems are there? *American Psychologist, 40,* 385–398.

Tversky, B. (1995). Cognitive origins of conventions. In F. T. Marchese (Ed.), *Understanding images* (pp. 29–53). New York, NY: Springer-Verlag.

Tversky, B. (2001). Spatial schemas in depictions. In M. Gattis (Ed.), *Spatial schemas and abstract thought* (pp. 79–111). Cambridge, MA: MIT Press.

University of Maryland, Baltimore County. (n.d.). *Managing discussions using a "participation portfolio."* Division of Information Technology. Retrieved from http://doit.umbc.edu/itnm/managing-discussions/

University of Northern Arizona e-Learning Center. (2016). *Using rubrics to grade online discussion.* Retrieved from https://www2.nau.edu/d-elearn/support/tutorials/discrubrics/discrubric.php

University of Wisconsin, Green Bay. (n.d.). *Sample discussion rubrics.* Retrieved from http://www.uwgb.edu/catl/files/workshops/business/samplerubrics.pdf

Vandervelde, J. (2016). *Online discussion rubric.* University of Wisconsin, Stout. Retrieved from https://www2.uwstout.edu/content/profdev/rubrics/discussionrubric.html

Vatz, R. E. (2016). The academically destructive nature of trigger warnings. *First Amendment Studies, 50*(2), 51–58.

Vekiri, I. (2002). What is the value of graphical displays in learning? *Educational Psychology Review, 14*(3), 261–312.

Vella, J. (2002). *Learning to listen, learning to teach: The power of dialogue in educating adults* (Rev. ed.). San Francisco, CA: Jossey-Bass.

Vella, J. (2008). *On teaching and learning: Putting principles and practices of dialogue education into action.* San Francisco, CA: Jossey-Bass.

Vygotsky, L. (1978). *Mind and society.* Cambridge, MA: Harvard University Press.

Wandersee, J. (2002). Using concept circle diagramming as a knowledge mapping tool. In K. Fisher, J. Wandersee, & D. Moody (Eds.), *Mapping biology knowledge* (pp. 109–126). Dordrecht, The Netherlands: Springer Netherlands.

Warren, L. (2005). Strategic action in hot moments. In M. Ouellett (Ed.), *Teaching inclusively: Resources for course, department, & institutional change in higher education* (pp. 620–630). Stillwater, OK: New Forums Press.

Watson, L. W., Terrell, M. C., & Wright, D. J. (2002). *How minority students experience college: Implications for planning and policy.* Sterling, VA: Stylus.

Weaver, R. R., & Qi, J. (2005). Classroom organization participation: College students' perceptions. *The Journal of Higher Education, 76*(6), 570–601.

Weimer, M. (2011, July 7). How much should class participation count towards the final grade? *Faculty Focus.* Retrieved from http://www.facultyfocus.com/articles/how-much-should-class-participation-count-towards-the-final-grade/

White, K. R. (1974). T-groups revisited: Self-concept change and the "fish-bowling" technique. *Small Group Behavior, 5,* 473–485.

White, S. W., Elias, R., Salinasa, C. E., Capriolaa, N., Connera, C. M., Asselinb, S. B., . . . Getzel, E. E. (2016). Students with autism spectrum disorder in college: Results from a preliminary mixed methods needs analysis. *Research in Developmental Disabilities, 56,* 29–40. doi:10.1016/j.ridd.2016.05.010

Whitt, E., Nora, A., Edison, M., Terenzini, P., & Pascarella, E. (1999). Women's perceptions of a "chilly climate" and cognitive outcomes in college: Additional evidence. *Journal of College Student Development, 40*(2), 163–177.

Wickens, C. D. (2002). Multiple resources and performance prediction. *Theoretical Issues in Ergonomic Science, 3*(2), 159–177. Retrieved from http://hci.rwth-aachen.de/tiki-download_wiki_attachment.php?attId=51

Wickens, C. D. (2008). Multiple resources and mental workload. *Human Factors, 50*(3), 449–455. Retrieved from http://www.researchgate.net/publication/23157812_Multiple_resources_and_mental_workload/file/3deec518144760291a.pdf

Wieman, C. E. (2007). Why not try a scientific approach to science education? *Change: The Magazine of Higher Learning, 39*(5), 9–15.

Wiggins, G. J., & McTighe, J. (1998). *Understanding by design.* Alexandria, VA: Association for Supervision and Curriculum Development.

Williams, B., Foster, L. N., Krohn, K. R., McCleary, D. F., Aspiranti, K. B., Nalls, M. L., & Quillivan, C. C. (2009). Increasing low-responding students' participation in class discussion. *Journal of Behavioral Education, 18*(2), 173–188. Retrieved from http://works.bepress.com/bob_williams/1/

Zhang, M. (2013). Fishbowl to roundtable discussions. *College Teaching, 61*(1), 39.

ABOUT THE AUTHORS AND CONTRIBUTORS

Authors

Jennifer H. Herman, director of the Center for Excellence in Teaching and associate professor of practice in education at Simmons College, develops and facilitates research-based faculty development opportunities around teaching and scholarship and provides structured support for curriculum design at all levels. She has been a grant co–principal investigator or curriculum designer on many high-impact initiatives, including open-source assessment modules for the National Institute of Learning Outcomes Assessment (NILOA), programs for the U.S. Department of State, the New York State Small Business Development Center's online Entreskills program, and a STEM teaching institute for Harvard Medical School, and she designs and facilitates course design institutes and inclusive excellence seminars. Herman received her PhD in higher education from the University at Buffalo and her MA in international training and education from American University. Her e-mail is jennifer.herman@simmons.edu.

Linda B. Nilson, now retired, directed 3 faculty development centers at major research universities during her 28-year career. She also authored several books: *Teaching at Its Best: A Research-Based Resource for College Instructors* (Jossey-Bass, 2016), now in its fourth edition; *The Graphic Syllabus and the Outcomes Map: Communicating Your Course* (Jossey-Bass, 2007); *Creating Self-Regulated Learners: Strategies to Strengthen Students' Self-Awareness and Learning Skills* (Stylus, 2013); *Specifications Grading: Restoring Rigor, Motivating Students, and Saving Faculty Time* (Stylus Publishing, 2015); and with Ludwika A. Goodson, *Online Teaching at Its Best: Merging Instructional Design With Teaching and Learning Research* (Wiley, 2017). She has given more than 450 keynotes, webinars, and workshops at conferences, colleges, and universities nationally and internationally. After receiving her PhD from the University of Wisconsin–Madison, she was a sociology professor at the University of California, Los Angeles. Her e-mail is nilson@clemson.edu.

Contributors

Mary Ann Drury, LCSW (Licensed Clinical Social Worker), is adjunct faculty at Columbia University School of Social Work, where she teaches residential and online graduate-level courses on workplace policy, staff development, and management. In private practice, she is an executive coach, organizational consultant, and psychotherapist. She brings 20-plus years of occupational, business, and clinical knowledge to advising management and human resources professionals on a broad range of workplace issues: leadership, manager development, performance and productivity, conflict mediation, critical-incident response, violence prevention, employee well-being, and healthy workplace practices. In addition, she coaches and advises leaders and teams in social services, the arts, law, health care, financial services, and media and entertainment. Connect with her on LinkedIn or by e-mail at md2926@columbia.edu.

Mary Jo Festle is Maude Sharpe Powell Professor of History at Elon University, where she also serves as an associate director of Elon's Center for the Advancement of Teaching and Learning. She teaches a variety of courses in U.S. history, including first-year topics courses, surveys, and senior research seminars, all on topics related to gender, race, sexuality, sports, and oral history. She authored two books, *Playing Nice: Politics and Apologies in Women's Sports* (Columbia, 1996) and *Second Wind: Oral Histories of Lung Transplant Survivors* (Palgrave Macmillan, 2012). Her current scholarly interests focus on teaching history. She can be reached at festle@elon.edu.

Matthea Marquart, MSSW, is the director of administration of the Online Campus at Columbia University's School of Social Work (CSSW). CSSW's Online Campus serves students across the United States and offers both a clinical and a management program. Marquart teaches in the management program, preparing a new wave of nonprofit and human services leaders. In her administrative role, she leads a team focused on the quality of the program. She has worked in teaching and training since 1997 and in online education since 2007. She writes and presents regularly on topics related to education and training. Contact her on Twitter at @MattheaMarquart or via e-mail at msm2002@columbia.edu.

Mary Shapiro has taught organization behavior and leadership to undergraduates, students in the master of business program, and executives in the School of Management at Simmons College for 25 years. In 2014, she was appointed to the newly endowed Trust Professorship of Leadership

Development to develop a leadership platform for integration throughout the undergraduate program. As a faculty affiliate of the Center for Gender and Organizations, she researches and publishes in the areas of women and their careers, risk taking, and confidence. Her most recent book, *Leading Teams* (Harvard Business School Press, 2015), is a culmination of years of consulting with teams in organizations such as CVS, WebMD, Harvard University, and Partners Health Care. Contact her at shapiro@simmons.edu.

Jennifer W. Shewmaker is a professor of psychology, associate dean of teaching and learning, and the executive director of the Adams Center for Teaching and Learning at Abilene Christian University (ACU) in Abilene, Texas. She earned her BS from ACU and her PhD from Texas Woman's University, both in psychology. She is a nationally certified school psychologist who has worked with hundreds of families, children, teachers, and community organizations in her career. As founding director of the ACU Master Teacher Program, she helps faculty use research-based teaching practices and peer observation to promote greater student learning. Contact her at jennifer.shewmaker@acu.edu.

Billy Strean is professor in the faculty of physical education and recreation at the University of Alberta, where in 2008 he received the Rutherford Award for Excellence in Undergraduate Teaching. In 2011, Strean was one of 10 Canadians selected to join the prestigious 3M National Teaching Fellowship. Strean is a master somatic coach and a registered yoga teacher. He received his PhD from the University of Illinois. He can be reached at billy.strean@ualberta.ca.

Heather Townsend is associate professor of biology at the Community College of Rhode Island, where she teaches a variety of lab and lecture courses including Microbiology, Organismal Biology, and Cellular Biology. She is dedicated to offering new educational experiences for her students and has a sustained commitment to teaching excellence and innovation. She received her BS from the University of Rhode Island in animal veterinary science and her MS and PhD from the University of Florida in veterinary medical science. She can be reached at hmtownsend@ccri.edu.

Janelle DeCarrico Voegele is director of teaching, learning, and assessment in the Office of Academic Innovation and affiliated faculty in the Graduate School of Education at Portland State University. She has a doctorate in educational leadership with a focus on postsecondary, adult, and continuing education. Her current research includes pedagogical approaches and student learning experiences in partially online courses. She can be contacted at voegelej@pdx.edu.

David M. Wilson is an associate professor at Parkland College in Urbana-Champaign, Illinois, where he has taught biology and chemistry since August 2004. His professional interests include molecular dynamics simulations, molecular evolution, and educational research. He can be reached at dawilson@parkland.edu.

thereby maximizing the possibility that students will become self-regulated learners who take responsibility for their own learning." —*Saundra McGuire, Assistant Vice Chancellor (Ret.) & Professor of Chemistry, Louisiana State University*

Linda B. Nilson presents an array of tested activities and assignments through which students can progressively reflect on, monitor and improve their learning skills; describes how they can be integrated with different course components and on various schedules; and elucidates how to intentionally and seamlessly incorporate them into course design to effectively meet disciplinary and student development objectives.

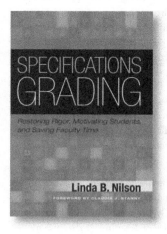

Specifications Grading
Restoring Rigor, Motivating Students, and Saving Faculty Time
Linda M. Nilson
Foreword by Claudia J. Stanny

"As an undergraduate, I often thought, 'After this course is over, I will learn the material,' feeling that traditional grading got in the way of my learning. Specifications Grading offers a practical alternative that increases student motivation to learn, self-direction, and mastery, while reducing grading time, grade grubbing, and student anger at constructive criticism. With myriad examples throughout, Specs Grading demonstrates how to make grading learning-centered, aligned with student-achieved learning outcomes, and civil."
—*Cynthia G. Desrochers, Professor of Education, Founding Director, Faculty Development Center, California State University, Northridge*

Linda B. Nilson puts forward an innovative but practical and tested approach to grading that can demonstrably raise academic standards, motivate students, tie their achievement of learning outcomes to their course grades, save faculty time and stress, and provide the reliable gauge of student learning that the public and employers are looking for.

22883 Quicksilver Drive
Sterling, VA 20166-2102   Subscribe to our e-mail alerts: www.Styluspub.com

Also available from Stylus

Hitting Pause
65 Lecture Breaks to Refresh and Reinforce Learning

Gail Taylor Rice

Foreword by Kevin Barry

"In this extraordinarily helpful book, Gail Rice provides two tremendous services to college faculty. First, she draws together research and arguments from a wide range of fields in order to demonstrate that simple, brief activities in class—built around the idea of creating "pauses" for student learning—can have a major positive impact on student success. Second, she presents a wealth of thought-provoking activities that faculty could begin using in their classrooms tomorrow. No faculty member will be able to read this book and not want to get immediately back into the classroom and put some of these excellent ideas into practice. An outstanding resource for faculty and those who work in faculty development." —*James M. Lang, Professor of English, Director of the Center for Teaching Excellence, Assumption College*

Pauses constitute a simple technique for enlivening and enhancing the effectiveness of lectures, or indeed of any form of instruction, whether a presentation or in an experiential setting. This book presents the evidence and rationale for breaking up lectures into shorter segments by using pauses to focus attention, reinforce key points, and review learning. It also provides 65 adaptable pause ideas to use at the opening of class, midway through, or as closers.

Creating Self-Regulated Learners
Strategies to Strengthen Students' Self-Awareness and Learning Skills

Linda B. Nilson

Foreword by Barry J. Zimmerman

"Linda Nilson has provided a veritable gold mine of effective learning strategies that are easy for faculty to teach and for students to learn. Most students can turn poor course performance into success if they are taught even a few of the strategies presented. However, relatively few students will implement new strategies if they are not required to do so by instructors. Nilson shows how to seamlessly introduce learning strategies into classes,

(Continues on preceding page)